MOMENTS OF
COURAGE

BRAVERY UNDER PRESSURE

Jay Jennings

Silver Burdett Press

Published by Silver Burdett Press, Inc., a division of Simon & Schuster, Inc.,
Prentice Hall Bldg., Englewood Cliffs, NJ 07632.

Designer: Greg Wozney
Manufactured in the United States of America
10 9 8 7 6 5 4 3 2 1

Library of Congress Cataloging-in-Publication Data

Jennings, Jay.
    Moments of courage : bravery under pressure / by Jay Jennings.
                  p.   cm. — (Sports Triumphs)
    Summary: Examines the lives and hard work of five athletes who
displayed courage in facing great obstacles.
    1. Athletes—United States—Biography—Juvenile literature.
2. Courage (Sports)—Juvenile literature. [1. Athletes. 2. Courage.]
                    I. Title.   II. Series
                    GV697.A1J454   1991
                    796′.092′2—dc20
[B]   90-47181
ISBN 0-382-24108-8 (lib. bdg.)
     0-382-24114-2 (pbk.)
                                                               CIP
                                                               AC

Cover photo: © Dan Helms from duomo

Acknowledgments

I would like to express my gratitude for the help and support given to me by my colleagues at *Sports Illustrated*. The work of Rick Telander, Demmie Stathoplos and Dan Levin was particularly helpful.

I send out special thanks to my patient and encouraging editor, Emily Easton; her pinch hitter, Adriane Ruggiero; and my agent, Kris Dahl, and her assistant, Gordon Kato, at International Creative Management.

As always, my wife, Jessica Green, provided the greatest support and inspiration.

Photo Acknowledgments

All Sport USA: Page 7 (All Sport/Tim De Frisco).
AP/Wide World Photos: Pages vi, 28, 31.
Carol L. Newsom: Page 46.
duomo: Pages 4, 9 (duomo/Dan Helms), 55 (duomo/Paul J. Sutton).
Focus on Sports: Pages 12, 16, 22, 32.
Gamma Liaison: Pages 34 and 43 (Jeff Schultz), 41 (Isabella Bich).
Map of the Iditarod: Robert Conrad.
Russ Adams Productions: Pages 52, 54.
Sports Illustrated: Page 20 (Lyn Pelham).

FROM THE AUTHOR

In the sports pages of newspapers or on the evening television sports report, we see the crucial moments of a game or event. A golfer sinks an important putt on the eighteenth green. With the bases loaded, a pitcher strikes out the other team's best hitter. A basketball player sinks a long shot to win the game as time expires.

These moments are exciting, but only rarely do they contain even a small element of courage. Skilled athletes display amazing physical feats every day. Most work very hard to master the physical and mental demands of their sports. But even a performance that sets a world record is not always a courageous one.

The athletes here all faced greater obstacles than the requirements of their individual sports. After experiencing the pain and danger of hitting his head on the diving board, Greg Louganis climbed back up the ladder to try again. Diana Nyad launched herself into a body of water no one had ever attempted to swim before. Fans and players yelled insults at Jackie Robinson, while pitchers hurled fastballs at him.

When courage is added to the difficulty of performing a sport at its highest level, the moments become something special, something worth preserving and recalling beyond the day's sports page.

These athletes faced enormous challenges. More often than not, the courage they displayed didn't exist just in that one moment but over the course of their lives. By reading about these brave people, perhaps we can learn to face our own difficult moments with just as much courage.

Jay Jennings

CONTENTS

In the 1988 Olympics, Louganis experienced a diver's greatest fear—hitting the board.

GREG LOUGANIS

Diving's Fearless Perfectionist

The best diver in the world stood on the board at the Chamshil Swim Stadium in Seoul, South Korea. He was going to attempt a reverse 2½ somersault *pike*, which required him to jump into the air and spin 2½ times back toward the board while hugging his straightened legs. Then he would release his legs and stretch out his body, entering the water headfirst.

It was only the *preliminary round*, and there was little pressure on him. Another round would determine the gold medal winner in the 1988 Olympics. Greg Louganis began his approach to the end of the board and took a small jump called the "hurdle step." The board bent toward the water. After the jump, he sprang up into the air to begin his spin. He completed one spin, then two, but as he straightened out to prepare for his entry into the water, he felt his head hit something hard. At the same time, he heard a dull *clonk*. The crowd at the stadium gasped. "Greg Louganis hit the board!" spectators said. "He hit his head!" Concern flooded through the crowd. "Is he hurt?"

Acting more out of instinct than anything else, Louganis reached for the water as controlled as usual. He climbed from the pool, rubbing the back of his head. Everyone was relieved. Still, when he felt his head and looked at his hand, he saw blood.

Louganis's injury wasn't serious. A doctor applied a temporary bandage to close the cut. But now, if Louganis wanted a gold medal, he had to climb the steps again and do two more dives. His head felt ok, but how would his mind be? Would he be too scared to really do his best? And if he did make it to the final round, he would have to perform the same dive again. How would he face the challenge the next time?

Louganis had been facing challenges all his life. His parents were only fifteen when he was born in 1960, and they gave him up for adoption. Peter and Frances Louganis adopted him when he was nine months old and took him to their home in El Cajon, California, which is near San Diego. They had already adopted a daughter, Despina. Peter Louganis worked for a fishing company in San Diego. Greg's biological father was from Samoa, an island in the Pacific Ocean. The Samoan people generally have smooth, dark skin and dark hair. Greg inherited these physical traits from his father. His biological mother was of British ancestry.

From his biological parents he also seemed to inherit a physical agility that started very young. He was already walking when the Louganises brought him home. Nine months later, he was tumbling and doing tricks like standing on his head. His sister Despina, who was three at the time, was taking a dance class. Mrs. Louganis enrolled Greg too. By the age of three, he was starring in a song-and-dance show. His mother made him a little tuxedo for the performance.

Throughout his early childhood, Greg continued to perform in musicals and dance shows. He added acrobatics to his activities and took part in competitions. He always had complete control over his body. The same was not true of his words. When he spoke, his mouth sometimes stalled on one sound. As hard as he tried, he could not end the stutter and make the sound come out of his mouth.

His sister, attempting to help him, would sometimes break in and finish the sentences for him. Mrs. Louganis disapproved of that. She thought Greg should not have to depend on his sister so much. After all, she would not always be around.

To overcome his stuttering, he entered a speech therapy class. By the time he reached the third grade, he was speaking without a problem. But he was still having trouble in class. When he looked at sentences in a book, the letters seemed jumbled and he could never be sure if he was getting the words exactly right. For example, the word "the" sometimes looked like "eth." If he was asked to read in class, he occasionally read the word "saw" for "was" or "god" for "dog." Since then, this common form of dyslexia—a physical reading problem—has become more widely recognized, but no one thought of it then. When he made mistakes, the class laughed. Louganis told Peter Michaelmore in *Reader's Digest*, "The other kids said I was retarded, and I thought I was." Some students called him names. Along with his reading problem came a loss in self-confidence. He became shy, withdrawn, and hesitant to speak out in class.

In dance or gymnastics class, he didn't have any fears. He felt comfortable and confident, as if he could do anything. When Greg was nine, the Louganises built a swimming pool in their backyard. Greg began jumping off the diving board, trying out the flips and twists he had learned in his gymnastics classes. His parents decided that if he was going to do those moves, he'd better learn the right way to do them, so they enrolled him in a diving class at the Parks and Recreation Center in La Mesa, California.

All the acrobatic training and tumbling of his youth gave him a headstart in the sport. He quickly became the best in his class and one of the best of his age in Southern California. Even very early on, he noticed the similarities between dancing and diving, and he used some of the techniques he had learned in dance class to improve his diving. In dance, sometimes the instructor would turn out the lights and play the music while the students pictured the whole routine in their minds. Greg did the same thing with his dives, picturing the perfect dive in his mind and then trying to copy it with his body. An early coach stressed that diving was not just a sport but an art form, and Greg agreed.

Within two years he was competing in national meets. While he was enjoying athletic success, school was still a world of problems. In addition to the taunts he suffered because of his reading disability, he experienced prejudice because of his dark complexion. Some of the kids called him "nigger."

The place where he could escape from all of the trouble was the pool. Standing high on the diving board, he was alone, far away from the cruelty of others. And he was good. Competing at the Junior Olympics in Colorado Springs, Colorado, in 1971, Greg was spotted by Dr. Sammy Lee, a former diver and Olympic gold medal winner for the United States in 1948 and 1952. He thought at the time that the eleven-year-old Greg was the greatest diving talent he had ever seen.

For the next four years, Greg continued to improve as a diver and even finished as high as fifth in the senior national championship. When Greg was fifteen, one of the divers that Lee coached beat Greg in

a meet. Peter Louganis then asked Lee if he would coach Greg. Lee agreed. He thought that he could turn Greg into a good enough diver to compete in the Olympics within a year.

Lee, a doctor of Korean ancestry, also identified with some of Greg's problems out of the pool. When Greg told him that he had been taunted and teased because he was half-Samoan, Lee told Greg in return about the way people treated him because he was a Korean.

Travel to national diving competitions was expensive and Greg's parents were not wealthy, so Greg found ways to earn money. His father helped him get a job repairing nets that the tuna boats used. He opened a savings account with the money he earned.

In January of 1976, Greg moved into the Lee home and began to train for that year's Olympics in Montreal, Canada. The sixteen-year-old surprised everyone by winning both the springboard and platform events at the U.S. Olympic Trials.

International diving competitions are made up of two events, the springboard and the platform. The springboard is a flexible fiberglass board positioned three meters (just over nine feet) above the water. One end of the board is fixed in place and the other end extends over the pool. The amount of spring in the board can be adjusted by moving the fulcrum, the support in the middle on which the board rests.

For the platform event, the divers leap from a rigid, usually concrete, stand, which is ten meters (thirty-three feet) high.

In each event, seven judges score each dive on a scale of zero to 10, with 10 being the best. They look for height in the leap, speed of **rotation**, and the absence of a splash on the entry—as well as grace, symmetry, and beauty. Of the seven scores, the highest and lowest are left out. The remaining ones are added together and multiplied by a number called the "degree of difficulty." That total is then multiplied

---

POOL TALK

pike: a diving position in which the diver's legs are straight and body is bent at the waist.

preliminary round: an early round of competition in which a large number of divers compete to determine which ones will move on to the final round.

rotation: a complete turn of the diver's body in the air; a flip.

tuck: a diving position in which the diver holds his or her legs close to the chest with the knees bent.

tower: another name for the diving platform.

by three-fifths. The degree of difficulty, which goes up to 3.5, is determined by the sport's governing body and measures how hard a dive is to perform. A dive with a greater number of twists and somersaults is harder to control than a simple forward dive, so the former one receives a higher degree of difficulty.

For example, if a diver performs a back $3\frac{1}{2}$ somersault **tuck** from the springboard (a 3.3 degree of difficulty) and receives scores of 6.5, 6.5, 7.0, 5.5, 7.5, 6.0, and 6.5, his total for the dive would be 64.35. The scores of 5.5 and 7.5 are dropped, the sum of the other scores is 32.5, which, multiplied by 3.3, equals 107.25. Three-fifths of that total is 64.35.

In Montreal, Louganis went up against one of the greatest divers of all time, Klaus Dibiasi of Italy. Dibiasi was already a two-time gold medal winner. Despite Louganis's youth and inexperience in international competition, he qualified for the final round in both events.

Before the springboard competition, Louganis found himself distracted by a problem out of the pool. Lee was not granted admission to Louganis's workouts because he was not an official coach of the American team. Without Lee, Louganis lost his focus, finishing only sixth in the springboard.

By the time the platform event came around, Lee was able to attend the workouts and Louganis was more relaxed.

Dibiasi, who was known as the Blond Angel, was expected to win. Louganis gave him an unexpected challenge, and the two were nearly even through eight of the ten dives. Louganis's ninth dive was a hard one: a forward $3\frac{1}{2}$ somersault in the pike position.

He leaped from the platform high into the air, throwing his body forward into a spin. His knees were locked straight, his feet pointed, and his toes curled. He grabbed the backs of his knees with his hands and pulled his chest to his thighs, spinning

Louganis achieved his perfect form only through years and years of practice.

three times before he released and stretched out his arms to break the surface of the pool.

As he pulled out of the pike, he kept his head down and made his entry into the water while still spinning. His legs flipped over and made a large splash. The judges deducted points from Louganis's dive for his poor entry. Many of the judges gave him only a 5. Dibiasi surged ahead on his dive.

Louganis's last dive was one of the best of his early career, but it was not good enough to bring him close to the Blond Angel. Dibiasi nailed his last dive and took home the gold medal. Louganis earned the silver, and though he was only sixteen years old, he was deeply disappointed. He felt as though he had let down his family, his coach, himself, and his country.

Returning to his high school in El Cajon, Louganis was a celebrity, but not a happy one. He desperately wanted to fit in with some group, so he began hanging around with the kids who smoked and drank. They saw themselves as outcasts, and Louganis decided he belonged with them. He began to ignore his training, and his performance suffered. In 1977, he competed in only one major meet, the U.S. Indoor Championship, where he finished second in the platform and a dismal eleventh in the springboard.

About that time, Dr. Lee, at age 57, decided to cut back on his coaching. Ron O'Brien, who ran a diving camp in Alabama that Louganis had attended when he was fifteen, took over the job of coaching the talented teenager.

O'Brien became not just a coach, but a friend to Louganis. O'Brien told *Sports Illustrated* magazine in 1981, "I don't have to coach him technically as much as the other divers because of his ability level. My main job is to keep him relaxed."

O'Brien succeeded from the start, and 1978 was the best year of Louganis's young career. He won both the one-meter springboard and the ten-meter platform titles at the U.S. Indoors. He also won the platform titles at the U.S. Outdoors and the World Aquatic Championships, which Dibiasi had won the year before.

In high school, Louganis had managed to compensate for his reading disability enough to figure out what most of the jumbled words said. As a result, his reading scores were high enough that he could attend college. The University of Miami, among many other schools, offered him a diving scholarship, and he chose to go there because of the university's excellent drama department. He knew that he could not dive forever, and he wanted to be an actor after his athletic career was over.

The schools in the National Collegiate Athletic Association, of which Miami was a member, don't have platform competition in their meets, so Louganis was forced to concentrate on the springboard.

In Miami, he began to feel better about himself. People weren't teasing him any longer. He became more than just a diver. His drama friends didn't know he was an Olympic medalist, and he liked that. They saw him as just another drama student.

At the same time, he discovered the secret of his reading problem. During his studies in freshman year, he came across a vocabulary word he hadn't seen before: dyslexia. He looked it up in the dictionary and found that the definition matched his problem perfectly. He was overjoyed to learn that he wasn't the "dummy" the kids had called him. His problem had a name, and he began to undergo reading therapy to overcome it.

Meanwhile, in the pool, he was enjoying greater success than ever before. At the Pan American Games in 1979, he won both the three-meter springboard and the ten-meter platform gold medals.

Visiting Russia that same year for a dual meet against the Soviet Union, Louganis's career almost came to a crashing halt. The platform at the meet was made of plywood instead of concrete and the divers were finding that their takeoffs had more spring in them than normal.

Louganis's third dive was a reverse pike, which required him to flip back toward the board after he jumped out over the water. The bounce of the plywood threw him off a bit, and as he straightened out for his descent, his head hit the platform with a *crack*. He fell limply into the pool far below, landing on his back.

Quickly, bystanders fished him from the pool. He was unconscious for almost fifteen minutes, but he was not badly hurt. He suffered only a concussion and a bruised back.

Three days after his accident, he was back in the pool in Miami. He had performed the reverse dive safely hundreds of times before, and he knew the best way to overcome a fear is to face it. His coach from Miami, Steve McFarland, was watching as Louganis climbed the platform to attempt the dive again. He took the position for the dive at the end of the platform and extended his arms in front to steady himself and prepare for the dive. The coach looked up nervously. Louganis jumped high into the air, but not out over the water! He was directly above the platform! His coach gasped. Then Louganis turned a complete back somersault, landing perfectly on his feet, solidly on the platform. Louganis laughed at the scare he had given the coach. With that kind of confidence, there was no doubt that he had conquered his fear of hitting the board.

Louganis finished out the year with victories in the platform events at both the U.S. Outdoors and the World Cup international meet. He was favored to win gold medals in both the springboard and the platform at the 1980 Olympics in Moscow.

He never got the chance. President Jimmy Carter called for a boycott of the Olympics in protest of the Soviet military invasion of Afghanistan. For Louganis and for hundreds of other American athletes, the wait for Olympic gold would last another four years.

Before beginning the task of preparing for an event four years away, Louganis took some time off to concentrate on classes at the University of California at Irvine. He had transferred there from Miami in order to be closer to Coach O'Brien. Interested in dance almost from the time he could walk, Louganis took a ballet class. He had never done anything more difficult. He told *Sports Illustrated*: "On the **tower** I do a few dives and I'll be a little sore the next day. From a ballet session, I come home dying, absolutely exhausted."

He also threw himself back into diving and quickly regained his championship form. In 1982, he won both the springboard and the platform at the World Championships, something no one had ever done before. At that same meet, he received 10s from all seven judges for one of his dives—a first for international competition.

But Louganis wasn't satisfied with staying at the same level of excellence. The other divers were getting better and he had to keep improving to stay ahead. O'Brien pushed him to try more difficult dives. One of these was a new dive, recently approved by international diving officials. It was a reverse 3½ somersault tuck. The diver stands at the edge of the platform, jumps out, pulls his legs into his chest and spins back toward the platform 3½ times before entering the water! Its degree of difficulty was 3.4, the highest of any platform dive. Louganis immediately added it to his list of dives and began working to perfect it. He always liked to save the most difficult dives for last in his routine in case he needed to make up points on another diver.

Few divers in the world had attempted the reverse 3½ before the 1983 World University Games in Canada. During the practices in the week before the meet, one Soviet diver had come dangerously close to hitting his head as he performed it. When the Soviet diver was scheduled to perform it in competition, Louganis was waiting his turn on the platform below. He never liked to know what any of the other divers were doing, so he turned his back to the pool and covered his ears with his hands.

The Soviet diver leaped out, but during his second somersault, his head hit the edge of the concrete platform. Standing below, Louganis felt the tower shake. He knew something terrible had happened.

The Soviet diver was unconscious when they pulled him from the water and rushed him to the hospital. His skull was fractured. After a 30-minute delay,

In the pike position, Louganis used the flexibility he acquired from dance classes.

competition resumed. When it was Louganis's turn to perform the same dive, he made sure that he jumped far out over the water and didn't come close to the tower.

A week later, the Soviet diver died of the injuries suffered at the meet.

The accident was disturbing for every diver, but Louganis didn't let it change the way he performed. He studied tapes of the dive to make sure he would never make the mistake the Soviet diver did. He accepted that the risk of injury is present in any sport but realized that if he was careful and sure of himself, he could minimize the danger.

He continued to chase his dream of an Olympic gold medal.

Away from diving, he was still not completely happy. He still smoked and drank as if he were trying to destroy his body rather than control it. One day at a meet, he saw a young diver puffing on a cigarette. Louganis asked him why he was smoking. "Because I want to be like you," the young diver said. The comment shocked Louganis. He saw clearly for the first time that his actions influenced others, and he decided to quit the foolish habits he had taken up.

In the pool, his quest for excellence continued. In 1983, he again won two gold medals at the Pan American Games and at the World Cup. He was coming as close to perfection as any diver had ever come.

As the 1984 Los Angeles Olympics approached, expectations for Louganis were high. He was generally acknowledged as the best diver in the world, maybe the best in the history of the sport. Everyone was watching him closely. His one fear was that he had already done the dives as well as he could.

He didn't have to worry. He won the springboard competition by 92.10 points, a margin so great he could have skipped his last dive and still won the gold medal.

He also outdistanced his rivals in the

platform competition, but there was still enormous pressure. Going into the last dive, he had a chance to become the first diver in history to top 700 points from the platform. The dive was the reverse 3½ somersault, the one that had killed the Soviet diver.

He stood on the platform, deep in thought. The eyes of the crowd were on him. What if he came close and didn't break 700? Would he ever be able to get that close again? And if he didn't, would people consider him a failure?

Then he had one thought that always calmed him: "No matter what happens, my mother still loves me."

He nailed the dive, ending with 710.91 points. He had become the first man since 1928 to win two diving gold medals in one Olympics and the first diver in history to break 700.

After the Olympics he began to do appearances and speak to groups about his dyslexia and his drinking. He warned students about the dangers of drugs and urged them to pour their energies into sports and creative activities.

Because of his busy speaking schedule, his diving fell off. He had decided he wanted to enter the 1988 Olympics and now he was finding himself pushed by younger divers. The low point of his diving career came in 1987, when he finished second in all three events—the one-meter springboard, the three-meter springboard, and the ten-meter platform—at the U.S. Indoor Championships.

He decided to cancel most of his speaking appearances and concentrate on preparing for the 1988 Olympics in Seoul.

By the time the Olympics came around again, Louganis was once more in top form. His biggest challenge would come from the young divers of China. The best of them were Tan Liangde and Xiong Ni. Xiong was only fourteen years old, half Louganis's age!

Louganis was not bothered by the stiff competition and was cruising through the preliminary round.

Then he sprung into the air on his reverse 2½ pike and smashed his head on the board. Though he got out of the pool without help, he was rattled. The blow came as a total shock to him. He said later, "I honestly didn't realize I was that close." How would the mishap affect his confidence? Would he be able to concentrate? Shortly after the doctors had placed the patch on Louganis's head, O'Brien took him aside and joked with him that hockey players get stitches all the time and still play, so he could go out there and do two little dives.

Louganis agreed but he was nervous. He had dropped from first to fifth in the standings. With the crowd applauding wildly, he performed a reverse 1½ somersault with 3½ twists. His score was 87.12, the best of the preliminaries. His last dive was also a good one and he raised his rank to third.

The next day, his jaw was a little sore from the accident. He told his manager that he felt like he had been hit by boxer Mike Tyson. Then he met with O'Brien, who counseled him during an early morning training session. He told Louganis that his mistake had been that he had jumped too far straight up and not far enough out over the water. He reminded Louganis that he had done the dive hundreds of times before without any problems.

When the final competition began, the swim stadium was packed with 5,000 spectators. Everyone wanted to see how Louganis would respond to his injury and to the challenge from Tan.

After five dives, Louganis held a 9-point lead over Tan. The lead grew to nearly 20 points after the next three dives. The crowd waited tensely for Louganis's ninth dive, the one during which he hit his head in the preliminaries. By that time he was 20 points ahead of Tan, not enough of a lead to relax.

Louganis stood on the board, rubbing his

face and breathing deeply. He walked out to the edge of the board, took his hurdle step, and sprung into the air. He was clear of the board, spinning in rapid revolutions. He came out of the position perfectly and reached for the water, entering with just a tiny splash. The crowd erupted. It was a beautiful dive. The judges gave him scores of 8s and 9s, and he retained his lead.

With that pressure gone, Louganis aced his last two dives to win the gold medal. *Sports Illustrated* called his effort "without question the crowning performance of a brilliant career."

But he still had to compete in the platform. There, his strongest competitor would be Xiong, the teenager from China.

The gold medals Louganis won at the 1988 Olympics were the crowning achievement of a great career.

Louganis found himself in a diving duel. Xiong was matching him dive for dive.

Going into his last dive, Louganis was 3 points behind Xiong. As he climbed the tower, he was set to conclude his program, and his Olympic career, with that most difficult and dangerous of dives, the reverse 3½ somersault pike. Twelve years earlier, Klaus Dibiasi had had to hit his last dive to defeat a teenaged Louganis. Now Louganis was in the same position.

Louganis wasn't thinking of the score. In fact, he didn't know if he was ahead or behind. He just wanted to do the best dive he could. He wasn't competing against Xiong. He was facing himself.

Standing at the edge of the platform, he reminded himself, as he had four years before, that his mother would love him no matter what he did. He exploded from his perch and kicked his straightened legs high into the air. He rotated through one, two, three revolutions, then extended his body as straight as a spear into the water.

When he climbed from the pool, he was smiling. He knew he had done his best, but would the judges agree?

The scores flashed up on the board. He was awarded one 9.0, five 8.5s, and an 8.0. The final scoreboard read:

Xiong 637.47
Louganis 638.61.

He had won the gold medal by little more than a point!

He fell, crying, into Ron O'Brien's arms. For the final time in his career, the world's best diver had the gold medal placed around his neck.

Even if Louganis had not won the gold medal, he had proven himself to be a courageous man. When he climbed up the ladder to the board after hitting his head, he showed that he was willing to face his fears. For that courage, he was rewarded with more than a gold medal. He gained the knowledge that no problem was great enough to make him quit.

GREG LOUGANIS

CAREER RECORD

Year	Competition	Finish in Event Three-Meter Springboard	Ten-Meter Platform
1988	Olympic Games	1st	1st
	U.S. Olympic Trials	1st	1st
	U.S. Outdoors	1st	1st
	Pre-Olympic Meet	1st	DNC
	Speedo Classic	1st	2nd
	McDonald's International	2nd	DNC
	U.S. Indoors	2nd	1st
	Drake International	2nd	1st
	Australia Day	1st	1st
1987	Pan American Games	1st	1st
	U.S. Outdoors	1st	1st
	Olympic Festival	1st	1st
	Bolzano International	1st	1st
	Volksbank International	1st	2nd
	McDonald's International	1st	1st
	FINA World Cup	1st	DNC
	U.S. Indoors	2nd	2nd
1986	Mission Bay Challenge	1st	1st
	U.S. Outdoors	1st	1st
	Olympic Festival	1st	1st
	World Championships	1st	1st
	McDonald's International	1st	5th
	U.S.A–U.S.S.R. Dual Meet	1st	1st
	U.S. Indoors	1st	1st
1985	U.S. Outdoors	1st	1st
	National Sports Festival	1st	1st
	U.S. Indoors	1st	1st

1984	U.S. Outdoors	1st	1st
	Olympic Games	1st	1st
	U.S. Olympic Trials	1st	1st
	USA International	1st	1st
	McDonald's International	1st	1st
	Australia International	1st	1st
	New Zealand International	1st	DNC
	U.S. Indoors	1st	2nd
1983	Pan American Games	1st	1st
	U.S. Outdoors	1st	1st
	L.A. 83 International	1st	2nd
	World University Games	1st	1st
	National Sports Festival	1st	1st
	USA International	1st	1st
	FINA World Cup	1st	1st
	U.S. Indoors	1st	2nd
1982	U.S. Outdoors	1st	2nd
	World Championships	1st	1st
	National Sports Festival	1st	1st
1981	U.S. Outdoors	1st	2nd
	National Sports Festival	2nd	1st
	FINA World Cup	2nd	DNC
	U.S. Indoors	1st	2nd
1980	U.S. Outdoors	1st	1st
	U.S. Olympic Trials	1st	1st
	USA International	2nd	DNC
	U.S.A.–China II	1st	1st
	U.S. Indoors	1st	3rd
1979	FINA World Cup	DNC	1st
	U.S. Outdoors	1st	1st
	Pan American Games	1st	1st
	National Sports Festival	1st	DNC
	U.S.A.–U.S.S.R. Dual Meet	1st	DNC
	USA International	DNC	3rd
	U.S. Indoors	1st	2nd
1978	World Championships	DNC	1st
	U.S. Outdoors	3rd	1st
	U.S. Indoors	27th	1st
1977	U.S. Indoors	11th	2nd
1976	Olympic Games	6th	2nd
	U.S. Olympic Trials	1st	1st
	U.S. Indoors	6th	2nd

DNC = Did Not Compete

Nyad's determination, both in and out of the water, helped her reach goals others thought impossible.

DIANA NYAD

Swimming's Marathon Master

Diana Nyad stood on the shore at Ortegosa Beach, Cuba, about 50 miles west of Havana. She looked straight in front of her, and all she saw was water. Her destination was Key West, Florida, 130 miles to the northeast. Sharks, jellyfish, and stingrays populated the ocean she would soon enter, undertaking an historic swimming feat. She hoped to do what no man or woman had ever done. She was going to swim those 130 miles, twice as far as anyone had ever swum in open water.

For eight years she had devoted herself to marathon swimming, first as part of an organized group of swimmers and later on her own. She had traveled around the world, swimming in every body of water imaginable—rivers, oceans, lakes, and seas. But even her greatest admirers questioned her sanity this time. She didn't care. They had called her crazy before for attempting other swims, but when she emerged on land at the end of her journey, they called her courageous. As in the past, she followed her own heart instead of listening to others. She was ready. Turning to the crowds behind her, she said, "I guess I'll see you all in about two and a half days." Then she walked out into the ocean until the water was waist deep. She dived in and began stroking.

Diana Nyad was born Diana Sneed on August 22, 1949, in New York City. When she was three, her parents divorced. Her mother then married a Greek land developer named Aristotle Zason Nyad, and the family moved to Fort Lauderdale, Florida. Though that marriage ended eight years later, Diana kept her stepfather's name.

The name proved prophetic. "Nyad" comes from the Greek word "naiad," which in Greek mythology was a nymph who lived in and presided over bodies of water. Diana took to the water early but didn't take up competitive swimming until the seventh grade, when a geography teacher encouraged his students to come out for the junior high swim team.

The teacher was Jack Nelson, who was also the swim coach at the school and a notable swimmer himself. He finished fourth at the 1956 Olympics in the 200-meter **butterfly**. Nelson was happy to see Diana come out for the team because he saw that she had a physique suitable for swimming: a very strong upper body, and slender hips and legs. He decided she would be a good backstroker.

With his encouragement, she became single-minded about swimming. She would work out in the morning for two hours starting at dawn or before and for two hours in the afternoon after classes. Soon she was one of the best swimmers in the state. In the ninth grade, she finished second in the 200-meter backstroke at a Florida senior regional championship. For the next three years she won the 100-meter backstroke at six state meets. For four straight years, she was selected captain of the swimming team.

All during high school, her primary goal was to compete in the Olympics. Winning a gold medal meant being the best in the world, and she wanted to be the best at whatever she did. She worked as hard as she could toward that goal.

One day in the spring of her junior year, as she was preparing for the nationals, she began having chest pains. She didn't want anything to interfere with her swimming season, so she didn't tell anyone. The attacks kept coming and soon she couldn't hide the pain. During practice one day Nelson found her clutching the side of the pool, doubled over in agony.

Doctors did a heart examination to find out what was wrong. They told Diana that she had developed a virus of the heart called endocarditis. Because the virus had reached the heart, it couldn't be treated with medication.

The only remedy was to rest in bed until the virus left the body. Diana hated to give up her swimming, but she followed the doctors' advice. For three months, she rested, reading all day and talking to her mother, sister, and brother. She lost a lot of

---

WATER TALK

buoys: floating markers in the water.

butterfly: a stroke in which the swimmer, positioned face down, propels himself or herself forward by throwing both arms in front out of the water and pulling them back to his or her sides under the water.

support boat: the boat providing a marathon swimmer with food and emergency help.

wake: the trail of moving water a swimmer leaves behind.

---

weight and strength.

In the fall, her heart was back to normal and she was able to work out again. But she wasn't the same. Her desire to be the best had not diminished, but she wasn't as fast in the water anymore. She had to face the fact that she would never make the Olympic team.

She thought she was through with swimming. Always an excellent student, she enrolled at Emory University in Atlanta, Georgia, and began studying to be a surgeon. Without the discipline and release of swimming, however, she began to find other, less productive outlets for her energy. She developed a reputation at Emory as a prankster. She was lucky to escape from one of her pranks alive.

During her sophomore year, she went to an Army-Navy surplus store and bought a parachute. With the parachute strapped to her back, she jumped from the fourth-floor window of her dormitory. In her book *Other Shores*, she called the stunt a "desperately crude, immature, and exhibitionistic cry for attention." The parachute worked and the only injury she suffered was a bruised heel, but the dean of women called her in to discuss her future at Emory. The talk did not go well. Soon after, she was asked to leave the university.

She took some time off from school, working as a lifeguard and a waitress. She told *Sports Illustrated*, "It was kind of scary being kicked out of college. I wasn't ready for a life of work yet." She began to apply to other schools, and a friend suggested Lake Forest College in a suburb north of Chicago, Illinois.

In spite of the troubles she had at Emory, she was admitted to Lake Forest. She was no longer interested in studying medicine, and she switched her area of study from science to English and French. She also started swimming in competitions again and performed well in regional meets, but she was still not able to regain the speed she had before her heart disease.

During her first semester at Lake Forest, she received a call from a man named Buck Dawson, who knew Nyad from Fort Lauderdale. He was director of the Swimming Hall of Fame, which is located there. He knew that Nyad loved swimming and that she was disappointed by her loss of speed. He also knew that she was a hard worker with good stamina. He thought she should try the marathon swimming circuit, in which swimmers traveled to the world's lakes, rivers, and oceans and competed in long distance races.

After speaking with Dawson, Diana decided to work as a counselor at the summer swimming camp he ran in northern Ontario, Canada. There she would begin training for the circuit.

During that summer, Dawson taught her the history of marathon swimming. She also entered her first race, a 10-mile open water swim in Lake Ontario. Some of the best long distance swimmers in the world were there.

In that very race, she quickly learned some of the tactics of the sport. As she surged out ahead of the pack, a swimmer from Egypt named Abdul Latif Abou-Heif followed closely in the **wake** she created. The technique, called "catching a ride," makes the work of the following swimmer easier because the leader breaks through still water, creating a kind of path for the trailing swimmer to follow.

Despite her inexperience, Nyad was the first woman to finish at the Lake Ontario swim (behind nine men) and even set a women's world record for the 10-mile distance with a time of 4 hours and 23 minutes. It was the greatest distance she had ever swum. She was thrilled by the challenge of the sport and was encouraged by her success.

Her next race was more difficult. The swim in Ontario was around a course of **buoys** which formed a half-mile lap. The next one started at Chicoutimi, Quebec, Canada, and covered 28 miles down a river, around a rocky shoreline, and into a bay. The year before, none of the swimmers who started the race finished. And they were the best in the world.

After 14 miles, Nyad was in 2nd place to Argentina's Horacio Iglesias, then the world's top distance swimmer. Twenty-two miles into the race, Nyad miscalculated a route and was swept into a bad tide that made her work hard just to keep from losing ground. The other swimmers avoided her mistake and passed her. She finally saw it was hopeless to continue, and Dawson pulled her to safety in the **support boat**. She was disappointed, but it was only her second competition. Only three swimmers finished the race at all.

At Chicoutimi the next year, she finished 7th with a time of 8 hours and 46 minutes. From 1971 through 1974, Nyad traveled around the world competing on the distance swimming circuit. She set women's world records for the 22-mile race from Capri to Naples, Italy, in the Bay of Naples; for the 26-mile race in the Parana River in Argentina; and for the 50-mile swim from the Great Barrier Reef to the coast of Australia. She set world records for both men *and* women in the north-to-south crossing of Lake Ontario. She has also swum in the Suez Canal and the Nile in

Nyad attempted to swim distances that no other swimmer—man or woman—had ever braved.

Egypt, the North Sea, the Caribbean Sea, and the Coral Sea. In 1974, she won the women's world championship in marathon swimming, in which points are accumulated by finishing high in the various competitions.

The demands of marathon swimming are grueling. Sometimes the swimmers have to be helped from the water. It is not unusual for a distance swimmer to lose twenty pounds during a swim. The effort also uses up many of the nutrients the body needs, so a trainer or several trainers follow the swimmers in a boat and feed them hourly doses of sugar-rich foods and liquids. Without these, the swimmers would not have the energy to finish the swim.

Preparation for a long distance swim is very important. Because the sun beats down continuously on the swimmers, they must be sure to have a deep bronze tan or some protection from the rays. In addition, the swimmers "grease up" before they enter the water, coating themselves with all kinds of goop from axle grease to plain Vaseline. This helps the swimmer glide more easily through the water and also provides warmth against the cold. Nyad generally used a combination of 90 percent lanolin (a fatty substance obtained from wool) and 10 percent paraffin (an ingredient in candle wax).

A disciplined training program is the most important preparation. During the marathon swimming season from January to October, Nyad worked out about five hours a day Monday through Friday. During those times, she would stay in a pool doing a couple of hours of middle distance (200, 400, 800, and 1,000 meters), an hour or so of sprints (50 and 100 meters), and then alternating slow and fast distances. On the weekends she would do distance work in the open water or a pool, often swimming for eight straight hours. She also worked weight training into the schedule.

As her career progressed, Nyad gradually came to see that her most difficult foes were not the other marathon swimmers but herself and the water. This became apparent to her in 1974 during a training swim, when she was pulled nearly unconscious from the frigid 40-degree waters of Lake Ontario. The hands of the person who rescued her were a normal 98.6 degrees, and Nyad's body was so cold, his hands burned her skin.

After her recovery, she saw the lake's cold waters as a challenge. She wanted to cross its 32 miles in a solo swim. She wanted to show that she could conquer the lake that almost conquered her. The sport had ceased to be interesting to her for the competition with other swimmers. "What interests me about marathon swimming is that it tests the human spirit," she wrote in *Other Shores*. "The real issue is the strength of the human will and the ability to focus that will under the most unimaginable of circumstances."

To create those unimaginable circumstances, Nyad decided to make a *double* crossing. She would first swim from Canada to the U.S., north to south, something no one had ever done. Nyad's trainer, Cliff Lumsden, was one of the best marathon swimmers ever, and he said that no one had ever tried it that way because the currents were too tricky. After reaching the U.S. shore and taking a ten-minute rest, as marathon swimming rules specify, she would enter the water again and swim the 32 miles back across.

The weather was perfect on the day in

mid-August, 1974, when Nyad plunged into the waters of Lake Ontario. The water temperature was 72 degrees, much more pleasant than the 40-degree chill that sent her to the hospital. Her stroke was steady and strong. During her years in the sport, she had come up with a system for keeping track of her progress. She knew six hundred strokes would take her one mile. She swam one stroke per second, sixty per minute. By keeping that pace and counting her strokes, she always knew how far she had traveled and how far she had to go.

The counting not only allowed her to keep track of her distance, but also kept her mind focused. Sometimes she thought of simple rhythmical songs as she swam. "Row, Row, Row Your Boat" took eight strokes, so repeating the song in her mind seventy-five times made a mile.

At Lake Ontario, every hour she stopped for a few seconds to take a drink of glucose (a syrupy sugar to replace the sugar the body has used). Four hours into her swim, the smooth water became choppier. Three hours later, she was fighting six- and seven-foot waves. The water temperature was down to 63 degrees, and Nyad was shivering. She kept stroking.

Finally, after 18 hours and 20 minutes, she reached her destination on the southern shore. It was 1:20 A.M. At 1:30, she had to be back in the water for the return trip. She was exhausted but felt satisfied that she had accomplished what no other person—man or woman—had ever done. After her ten minutes were up, she was back in the water, returning the way she came. She didn't last long. Two hours into the return trip, she blacked out. Her support boat rescued her.

Nyad didn't consider the swim a failure, just because she didn't complete what she had set out to do. She wrote in *Other Shores*, "In my heart, the Lake Ontario swim was a success. Against near-impossible odds, I made it to the southern shore and had the courage to walk back into that frozen dark for the return trip."

The attempt did make her hungry to try other solo swims. The next year she began to make arrangements to swim around Manhattan island in New York. The challenge would not necessarily be the distance. It is 28 miles around the island, but three rivers flow together at the north end, and the currents and whirlpools can be strong and unpredictable.

Nyad spent days with the New York Coast Guard plotting out the best place and time to begin her swim. She decided to begin in the northeast section of the island at a place ominously called Hell Gate, where the Harlem, East, and Flushing Rivers flow together. Most successful swims started at the south end of Manhattan, but the record holder (Byron Summers in 1927) dove in at Hell Gate. If she started at low tide there, the whirlpools would be less dangerous, and since she was only beginning her swim, she would be at her strongest.

Despite her careful planning, during her first attempt she was defeated by the one thing she had no control over—the tides. After five and a half hours she had made it to the Battery, the lower tip of Manhattan. Next she had to turn the corner and swim up the East River. According to predictions, the ocean tides would push the current up the river in her favor and the water would be flowing with her at the time she arrived. Nyad swam out about 50 yards into the river and found she was going nowhere, no matter how hard she swam. The tides hadn't turned yet. She retreated to the seawall of the Battery.

Darkness fell as she waited for the tides to change. The water temperature dropped. She began to shiver. Ferries and boats sailed around her in the darkness, putting her in danger of being run over if she left the seawall. After an hour and a half of waiting, she didn't respond to shouts from her support boat. Stopping for so long had caused her to grow colder and colder. Her

trainers made their way to her and pulled her from the water.

She was rushed to Brooklyn Hospital where her body was covered with hot towels until her temperature rose to normal. Within an hour she was feeling better and talking about trying again.

That attempt was to come on October 6. New York and the nation became interested in her story. Everyone in the press kept asking her, "Why?" She answered, "If you want to know why I'm going to do it, I have no concrete answer. It's just that I have a personal and intimate psychological relationship with marathon swimming." At 65 degrees, the water was much colder than when she had tried before, so this time she covered her body with lanolin before entering. She lowered herself from the boat at Hell Gate, and pushed off at 11:35 A.M.

After an hour and a half, Yankee Stadium (the home of the New York Yankees baseball team) was on her right as she stroked steadily toward the Hudson River on the west side of the island. There was a lot of garbage in the water, and when she stopped every hour to eat, her goggles were clouded with scum.

The Hudson was rougher than usual, but she was swimming with the current, which made progress easier. At 5:05 P.M. she reached the Battery and would once again have to fight the East River and the tides that had stopped her before. This time, the tides had turned and were cooperating.

After inching around the Battery close to the seawall, she pushed off into the East River and headed for Hell Gate. Nothing would stop her this time. The evening was perfect, and as the rush-hour traffic lined the bridges above her head, Nyad continued pushing toward her goal. Completing the swim was not the only thing on her mind. She knew she had a chance to beat the record that Byron Summers had set.

Crowds lined the shore, cheering her on as she wearily stroked for the finish. At 7:32 P.M. she touched the wall from which she had pushed off. She had circled the island in 7 hours and 57 minutes, breaking the old record by 59 minutes.

There was another challenge waiting for Nyad, a bigger one than the swim around Manhattan. She wanted to do something no one had ever done before. She would swim from Cuba to the United States.

As with all her marathon swims in the past, preparation was one of the most important considerations for Nyad. For the Cuba swim, she decided to take at least a year to train and get ready.

Several factors made this the most difficult swim ever attempted. The first was sheer distance. No one had ever swum 130 miles in open water before without stopping. Nyad figured she would be in the water for two and a half days.

Other challenges abounded. The water in that area is rough and choppy. Waves would toss her around, perhaps adding seasickness to an already difficult feat.

The creatures in the water could be more dangerous than the water itself. Sharks roamed the area. In order to be protected from them, Nyad would have to swim within the confines of a specially built motorized cage. Jellyfish also were plentiful, and their tentacles could sting an unaware swimmer. Even sea gulls could get into the act, mistaking a swimmer for a surfacing fish and pecking at her head.

In July, 1977, a year before the Cuba swim, Nyad began her training. For eight months, she ran 10 to 12 miles every day at around a six-minute-per-mile pace, added weight training to that twice a week, skipped rope, and played squash. To keep her feel for the water, she occasionally swam a few laps in a pool.

At the end of February, she began to focus on the Cuba swim. She ended all land training except the weights and began swimming five hours a day. In April, she increased the swimming to six or eight hours a day. In May she moved to Miami to begin ocean swimming, spending up to

twelve hours at a time in the water. Nyad devoted the last month before the Cuba swim to several "warm-up" swims.

Unfortunately, problems with Cuba's government resulted in delays. The July starting date had to be pushed back to August when the conditions were not as good. Still, on August 13, she set off from Ortegosa Beach with the expectation of dragging herself onto the Florida shore some 60 hours later.

From the beginning, there were problems. When she entered the surf at 2:07 P.M., the water was choppier than normal because of the gusting winds. The winds continued for hours into her swim. Waves rocked the cage and hit Nyad in the face.

The winds continued to rage, blowing the cage off course to the west. They kept blowing far into the night. Jellyfish stung her repeatedly. She kept swimming. The waves grew to six feet. Still, she fought through them. After twelve hours, she was weary and seasick but not beaten. She continued swimming through the night.

The next morning, her seasickness had passed and she felt stronger, but the amount of time she had spent in the salt water was beginning to take its toll. Her lips were cracked from the wind, water, and sun and salt water stung the wounds. Her tongue was so swollen that she couldn't take her regular feedings.

All through the day, she kept churning through the rough water. She told her trainers she didn't want to know how far she had gone. The wind rose again that night and the waves sometimes reached seven feet. She was making little progress. Her mind began playing tricks on her. She saw lizards in the bottom of the cage at one point. She kept swimming through the second night.

Tuesday morning the waves grew to seven and eight feet. The navigator of the shark cage took a reading on their position and found they were far off course. Nyad had been swimming for forty-two hours and

For her swim from Cuba to Florida, Nyad constructed a cage to protect her from sharks.

had covered only a little more than 50 miles of her intended route. She had actually swum more than 75 miles, but because of the changes in course, she was still 80 miles from the finish. It was hopeless.

The navigator stepped onto a pontoon, one of the floating supports of the boat and told Nyad, who was still stroking away, "It can't be done, Diana." She refused to believe it and said, "I can't quit." Her voice was garbled because of her swollen lips and tongue. In her heart, however, she knew the truth. She would have to give up the swim.

Friends on the boat lifted her from the water. She told them, "I've never done anything so hard in my whole life."

Though disappointed by her failure to reach her goal, Nyad didn't look back with regret but looked ahead to another goal. She began planning a swim for the next year that would take her from the Bahamas,

a group of islands in the Atlantic Ocean, to the east coast of Florida. The straight distance was about 60 miles.

Again she undertook a tough training schedule, and by the first week in August, 1979, she was ready to plunge in. She left the beach at North Bimini Island and stroked for the coast. After only 12½ hours, she was removed from the water. Stings from jellyfish prevented her from continuing and even temporarily paralyzed her.

Amazingly, two weeks later she was back on the beach again, this time with a latex coating over her body to protect her against jellyfish. She entered the water just after 8 A.M. on August 19.

She started counting and singing her way to the Florida coast. The powerful Gulf Stream, a warm ocean current that flows from the Gulf of Mexico in the south to

Europe, pulled her off a straight-line course to the north. Its force had prevented other swimmers from completing the swim, but Nyad powered her way through without any problems.

Around dawn on August 20, in spite of her protection, a small jellyfish stung her. She was frustrated and cried out, "Why, why, why?" But she kept swimming.

Soon, the coast was in sight. She stroked harder, knowing that she could reach her goal. Hundreds of people were waiting for her on the beach at Jupiter, Florida, just about 50 miles from her home town of Fort Lauderdale.

The crowd cheered and cheered as she struggled out of the water. Even though she was exhausted, she was smiling broadly.

She had done it!

"Everybody said it couldn't be done!" she cried, and the crowd cheered some more.

Diana Nyad spent her career doing things that people said couldn't be done. She had looked across many bodies of water and seen a distant shore where others only saw impossibility.

FOR THE EXTRA POINT

Nyad, Diana. *Other Shores*. New York: Random House, 1976. (Advanced readers.)

McLenighan, Valjean. *Diana: Alone Against the Sea*. Milwaukee, Wisconsin: Raintree, 1982.

DIANA NYAD

Major Long Distance Swims

Date	Distance	Time (Hours:Minutes)	Start	Finish
August 20–21, 1979	89 miles	27:38	North Bimini Island, Bahamas	Jupiter, Florida
August 13–15, 1978	76.1 miles	41:47	Ortegosa Beach, Cuba	Straits of Florida
October 6, 1975	28 miles	7:57	Around Manhattan, New York City	
August, 1974	32 miles	18:20	Across Lake Ontario, Canada	
Summer, 1971	28 miles	8:46	Chicoutimi, Quebec, Canada	Bagotville, Quebec, Canada
July 26, 1970	10 miles	4:23	Lake Ontario, Canada	

Robinson's success opened the door for black players to have careers in the major leagues.

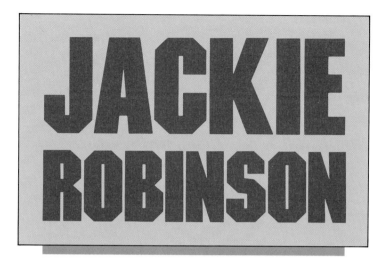

JACKIE ROBINSON

Breaking Baseball's Color Barrier

The 1947 baseball season was only a week old when the Philadelphia Phillies traveled to Ebbets Field to meet the Brooklyn Dodgers in a three-game series. Jackie Robinson was the first baseman for the Dodgers that day, as he had been on April 15, the team's Opening Day. On that day he had become the first black since the turn of the century to play in the major leagues.

For many years, organized baseball (the major league teams and their minor league affiliates) had followed an unwritten rule about black athletes. No blacks were allowed to play for any major or minor league team. As a result blacks played among themselves in what were called the Negro leagues.

In 1945, Robinson and Branch Rickey, the general manager of the Dodgers, decided to break the "color line" by signing Robinson to a professional contract. The signing created quite a controversy. Robinson knew it was a difficult but important burden to bear. He would be an example for his whole race. How he responded to the pressure would determine how soon other blacks would get the same chance.

Many people objected to the mixing of the races in baseball. They argued that the "Negroes" had their own leagues and should only compete against each other. Others supported the move, reasoning that if black soldiers had fought and died for freedom on the World War II battlefields, then black baseball players should be allowed to play in the major leagues.

His first week with the team was relatively calm. He went hitless in his first game but scored a run after he had reached base on a walk in a 5–3 Dodger win. He got his first hit in the second game and his first home run in the third.

When Robinson came up for the first time against the Phillies, a roar of racial slurs and angry comments sounded from the Philadelphia dugout.

There was one central figure behind the insult barrage. Philadelphia's manager was a man from Tennessee named Ben Chapman. He had ordered his players to taunt Robinson with the hope of distracting him and breaking his concentration so he wouldn't play as well. Almost all major leaguers experience this "bench jockeying" at some point in their career, but the cruelty of the abuse heaped on Robinson was far worse than it would have been for another player.

Robinson was a proud man who rarely backed down. Whenever he encountered racial prejudice, he had fought back.

Now he was being pushed to the very limits of his tolerance. How would he react? Would he fight back with his fists? His response would determine how quickly baseball's "noble experiment" would succeed.

Jack Roosevelt Robinson was born on January 31, 1919, near Cairo, Georgia. His father was a poor sharecropper, a farm worker who lives on another farmer's land and gives him a portion of the crop instead of rent. Shortly after Jackie, the youngest of five children, was born, his father abandoned the family. Jackie's mother, Mallie, was left to raise the family on her own.

She decided that they would be better off living in another place, and she moved her five children across the country to Pasadena, California. With the wages she earned as a maid and with the help of a welfare agency, she was able to buy a house on Pepper Street. Mallie Robinson and her children soon found out that they didn't escape prejudice when they left the South.

Their white neighbors on Pepper Street objected to the presence of a black family and petitioned to have the family removed. Mallie Robinson stood her ground and refused to collapse under the pressure. The neighbors offered to buy the home from her. She turned down the offer. Angered by Mallie's refusal to leave, the neighbors turned to name calling, rock throwing, and other forms of harassment. Still the Robinsons stayed.

The boys often answered the taunts with taunts of their own. The end result was usually a fight. Robinson wrote in his autobiography, *Baseball Has Done It*, "My brothers and I were in many a fight that started with a racial slur on the very street we lived on."

Sports headed off the road to juvenile delinquency for Jackie, his brothers, and their friends. They formed neighborhood teams and challenged other neighborhoods to games. The Robinsons were the stars at every sport—football, baseball, basketball, and track.

Their success continued into and beyond their teens. Jackie's brother, Mack, was a track star, and he even earned a spot on the 1936 U.S. Olympic team. At Berlin, Germany, he won a silver medal for finishing second behind the famed Jesse Owens in the 200-meter dash.

Today, such athletic success would almost surely mean money, fame, and the opportunity for a continuing athletic career. No such guarantee was present then, especially for a young black man. When Mack returned home from Berlin, he got a job with the Pasadena City government, but when a judge ordered the city to open its public swimming pools to blacks, the city responded by firing all its black employees, including Mack.

Jackie was an even better and more versatile athlete than his Olympian brother. First at Pasadena Junior College, then at the University of California at Los Angeles (UCLA), Jackie starred in football, basketball, baseball, and track. Sometimes when the seasons overlapped, he would compete in one sport in the morning and another in the afternoon. At UCLA, he was an All-American selection in football, and in basketball he twice led the Pacific Coast Conference in scoring. Surprisingly, baseball was his poorest sport in college; in 1940, he hit only .097.

Jackie loved sports and wanted to make them a career, but like his brother, he found few options open to him. Though he was a brilliant athlete in college, professional sports did not offer him opportunities. He dropped out of school to get a job and support his mother.

He worked briefly for a government agency called the National Youth Administration, which hired him to teach sports to disadvantaged kids. The government soon closed down the agency, and Jackie was out of a job. He also earned a little extra money and kept his own athletic skills in shape by playing semiprofessional football, first in Los Angeles and later in Hawaii.

On December 7, 1941, Jackie was on a boat returning to the U.S. mainland from Hawaii, when he heard that the Japanese had bombed Pearl Harbor. The attack triggered the entry of the United States into World War II. Jackie was drafted by the Army and assigned to Fort Riley, Kansas.

His time in the Army was marked by conflict over its racial policies at the time. Many of the bases were segregated, separated into white and black units, and the two didn't mix. Robinson, who had

fought discrimination all his life, wouldn't put up with the policies.

He applied to Officers' Candidate School for soldiers who demonstrated intelligence and leadership qualities. Though Robinson had a college background and seemed to satisfy all the requirements, he was not admitted to the school. Convinced that he was being discriminated against, he took his case to another black soldier at the base, Joe Louis, who was the heavyweight boxing champion of the world at that time. Louis contacted a friend who worked in the government, and the friend helped arrange for Robinson and other qualified blacks to enroll in the school.

Robinson ran into another problem when black soldiers in his battalion complained about the seating arrangements in the segregated dining hall. Black soldiers were forced to stand or wait for tables when there were free tables in the white section. When Robinson phoned another officer to relay the complaint, the officer, thinking Robinson was white, said, "How would you like to have your wife sitting next to a nigger?" Robinson erupted in anger, shouting over the phone to his superior. After taking his case to other higher ranking officers, Robinson eventually succeeded in changing the seating policy.

In athletics at Fort Riley, Robinson experienced more prejudice. He joined the base's football team, which was integrated and allowed blacks and whites to play together. The team played colleges and other bases. When the Fort Riley team was scheduled to play the University of Missouri, the coach at Missouri refused to field his team because of the base's black players. The Army solved the problem not by challenging the school's blatant discrimination, but by giving the black players leave so they could go home. Robinson took advantage of the unexpected leave to visit his family in Pasadena, but he was so angry at the Army's cowardice that he refused to play another game for the football team. In baseball, he was not even allowed on the team because it was all-white.

Robinson's fight against Army discrimination finally resulted in an incident which brought him to trial before a military court. He had been transferred to Fort Hood, Texas, where he had taken over a tank battalion. One day he hopped on a bus that served the base and took a seat near the front. The driver stopped the bus and told Robinson to sit in the back, where the seats were reserved for blacks. Robinson refused to move, since he knew that the Army had recently outlawed segregated seating on buses serving Army bases. The driver shouted that if Robinson didn't move, he would be in trouble. Robinson stayed where he was, yelling back that he knew his rights. At the end of the ride the driver called the military police, who asked Robinson to go with them to see the captain.

The captain was not sympathetic and soon Robinson was brought before a military court, which charged him with conduct unbecoming an officer. In court Robinson was cleared of the charge, but he'd had enough of the Army. He requested and received an honorable discharge in 1944.

Out of the Army, he turned again to the world of sports for his career. The Kansas City Monarchs, a Negro league baseball team, paid Robinson $400 a month to play for them. Giving the game his full attention and the full range of his athletic talents as he had never been able to do in college, Robinson soon excelled for the Monarchs in the field at **shortstop** and at the plate. He started at his position in the league's East-West All-Star Game and batted .340 for the season.

Despite his success, Robinson didn't enjoy life in the Negro leagues. In college he was used to playing on integrated teams against the best competition in the nation. College athletics were well organized and popular, while life in the Negro leagues was often unstructured and haphazard. Players traveled great distances by bus, and when they arrived in a city, they often found hotels and restaurants that served blacks to be dreary, run-down places. Teams sometimes dropped out of or joined the league in the middle of a season, and the schedules were always changing.

In spite of the conditions, some of the best baseball players of the day, including Robinson, competed in the Negro leagues. Leroy "Satchel" Paige was one of the greatest pitchers of all time and played for twenty-two years in the Negro leagues before he got the chance to pitch in the majors in 1948. Catcher Josh Gibson of the Pittsburgh Crawfords was a powerful hitter who, by all accounts, could have led any league in home runs.

DIAMOND TALK

brushback pitch: a pitch close to the batter, which forces him to back away from the inside of home plate.

bunt: a batted ball put into play directly in front of the home plate area when the hitter simply allows the pitched ball to strike it.

double play: a defensive play in which two outs are made on one batted ball.

exhibition game: a game between two teams which does not count in the official standings.

franchise: any team that is a member of a league.

roster: the list of players on the team.

shortstop: the position on the baseball field between second and third base.

strike zone: the area over home plate in which a pitched ball, if not hit by the batter, is called a strike. By current rules, the strike zone extends from the batter's armpits to his knees.

During that 1945 season, a scout for the Brooklyn Dodgers named Clyde Sukeforth was touring the Negro leagues looking for talent. He had been given the assignment by his boss, the general manager of the Dodgers, Branch Rickey.

He was a very shrewd man who knew the business of baseball. Earlier in his career with the St. Louis Browns he had invented the farm system, where a minor league team will train young, talented players for a single major league team. Later under Rickey, the St. Louis Cardinals became the most successful **franchise** in the National League.

When he joined the Brooklyn Dodgers in 1942, he had a more controversial plan for bringing talent to the team. He began to lay the groundwork for a plan that would bring black players into the league for the Dodgers. Rickey's crusade for an integrated league was not just an attempt to improve the talent of the Dodgers. He felt strongly that racial discrimination was morally wrong and that he should do whatever he could to combat it.

When he was the baseball coach at Ohio Wesleyan University in 1910, the team had a star player named Charley Thomas, who was black. The team traveled to South Bend, Indiana, for a game against Notre Dame, but the hotel would not let Thomas stay there. Rickey convinced the hotel management to let Thomas stay in Rickey's room. In the night, he heard Thomas rubbing his hands furiously and saying, "Black skin! Black skin! If only I could make them white." From that moment on, he pledged to himself that he would do all he could to end racial discrimination.

While he was at St. Louis, he knew the location and the team were not right for introducing black players to the major leagues. When he moved to Brooklyn, he thought that the melting pot of a city like New York would be more accepting of such a bold move.

He also knew that his decision would not be welcomed by all players and other team executives, so he thought very carefully about the best way to execute his plan. More important, he thought about the kind of man who would have to fill the role of the first black in major league baseball.

First of all Rickey knew that the man he chose to sign to a contract would have to have the skills to play in the majors. Though there were many talented players in the Negro leagues, some of the best were too old to begin a major league career. If the player was too young and his skills too raw to perform well in the majors, the opponents of integrated baseball might say that his failure meant blacks lacked the talent to play at that level.

More important than the actual skills was the personality of the player. Everyone would look at him as representative of all blacks. Rickey knew the player would have to be a model citizen on and off the field.

Rickey didn't know if such a man even existed, but he set about trying to find him. He hatched a plan that would keep his search a secret, until the proper moment when he could reveal his move. He told Dodger scouts that he was going to field a team called the Brooklyn Brown Dodgers in a new Negro league. He ordered his scouts to travel the country in search of players for the team.

They came up with several candidates, but one name kept coming back to Rickey more than the rest—Jackie Robinson, the shortstop for the Kansas City Monarchs. One scout called him the best **bunter** in baseball. Another said he was the best two-strike hitter he had seen in a long time. He had also been mentioned frequently in the black press as a possible candidate to break the major league color line.

Rickey traveled to California to look into the player's background. He liked what he found. Robinson was intelligent, having completed almost all of college. His college career had given him experience playing on integrated teams. He was a strict

Methodist who neither smoked nor drank, but he wasn't the kind of player who would back down when challenged.

Robinson still had to pass one more test for Rickey—a personal interview. Rickey flew him to the Dodger offices.

The two men met on August 28, 1945. They looked each other up and down for a few minutes. Rickey still wasn't sure that Robinson was his man, and Robinson wasn't sure why he was there. Rickey got right to the point, explaining that he didn't want Robinson to play for the Brown Dodgers, he wanted him for the Brooklyn Dodgers in the National League.

Robinson was stunned. This was the chance he had dreamed about, but he had no idea it would come so soon, if at all. Rickey told Robinson he would start out at the Dodgers' farm team in Montreal. Then Rickey acted out all the problems Robinson would face. For three hours, Rickey challenged Robinson by playing the roles of an insulting waiter, a bitter teammate, a cruel hotel clerk. Rickey yelled at him all the insults he could expect to hear. Hearing the names he had endured all his life, Robinson fumed inside but kept calm.

After a few minutes Robinson said, "Mr. Rickey, do you want a ballplayer who's afraid to fight back?" Rickey responded, "I want a player with guts enough NOT to fight back."

Launching into a final role, Rickey said, "Now we're in the World Series. I'm a player sliding into second with my spikes in the air. You take the throw and tag me out. I'm mad as hell, and all I can see is your black face, so I punch you in the cheek." At this, Rickey swung a fist just in front of Robinson's face. Robinson flinched then said, "I've got it. What you want me to say is that I've got another cheek."

Rickey knew that Robinson was talking about the Christian doctrine of answering violence with non-violence: "If any one strikes you on the right cheek, turn to him the other also."

Rickey then offered Robinson a contract to play professional baseball at Montreal. Robinson sat silent for a long time, then he said to Rickey, "If you want to take this gamble, I will promise you there will be no incident."

For two months, Rickey and Robinson kept the agreement secret. Then the Montreal Royals, for whom Robinson would play the 1946 season, called a press conference to announce the signing and reveal Rickey and Robinson's "noble experiment." For the five months before the start of the season, fans, players, writers, and executives debated the merits of the

Robinson and Branch Rickey, shown here in 1962, masterminded the plan to break baseball's color barrier.

move. Some predicted that it wouldn't work. Others gave their wholehearted support to the signing. So before Robinson had played a game in the major or minor leagues, everyone knew his name.

Robinson, for his part, was more concerned with his personal life. The money from his contract gave him the financial security to allow him to marry his longtime girlfriend from college, Rachel Isum. Two weeks after the wedding, they left California for Daytona Beach, Florida, where Robinson would participate in the Dodgers' spring training camp.

As a part of the Deep South, Florida restaurants, hotels, and public facilities were still separated into black and white sections. At the baseball parks where the teams played, blacks were allowed to watch the games only from special areas, usually the worst seats in the park.

For seven weeks, Robinson put up with the harsh realities of a segregated society. He was not allowed to stay at the same hotel with the other Dodger players, so he lodged with a local black doctor. At Jacksonville, a game between Montreal and Brooklyn was canceled when the city revealed a law that would not allow whites and blacks to compete on city-owned property. At Sanford, Florida, the chief of police walked onto the field during a game and informed the Montreal manager that Robinson had to leave the park.

The fans were more tolerant than the officials. As spring training progressed, they turned out in record numbers to see Robinson play. For the most part he was greeted with cheers, especially by the black fans who crowded into their sections. Robinson didn't disappoint them. He beat out bunts for base hits. Once on base, he distracted opposing pitchers with his quickness, taking off for the next base or faking a steal. The fans, black and white alike, loved the excitement he brought to the game.

The treatment of Robinson by some city officials and by those who supported segregation received widespread criticism and coverage in the newspapers that were there to cover Robinson's story. The bad publicity helped to change some attitudes or at least forced some communities and leaders to take a closer look at their policies of discrimination.

On the outside, Robinson emphasized that he was just there to play ball and wouldn't let the racial policies bother him. On the inside, he was tense and nervous from the pressure. Rachel Robinson later told Art Rust, Jr., in the book *"Get That Nigger Off the Field!"*, "He was trying too hard; he was overswinging; he couldn't sleep at night; he had trouble concentrating."

The pressure only became more intense as Robinson suited up for his first official game in organized baseball. Montreal opened the season in Jersey City, New Jersey, and the town and the baseball world were buzzing with excitement. The stadium was packed to capacity with twenty-six thousand people. Almost as many gathered outside the ball park.

As he stepped into the batter's box, his palms became damp and his legs felt as if they wouldn't hold him up. There were many black fans in the stands that day, most of them seeing a baseball game for the first time. They cheered when Robinson came up, but the applause they gave him was hardly deafening. Many of the whites in the stands sat still, waiting for Robinson to prove that he could play the game.

He ran the count to 3 balls and 2 strikes before hitting an easy ground ball to the shortstop, who threw him out. The pressure of the first at bat was off. Now maybe he could relax.

His next at bat came in the third inning. The Royals had two men on base. The pitcher wound up and threw a fastball, high in the **strike zone**. Robinson swung and connected, sending the ball with a crack over the leftfield fence. A home run!

He jogged around the bases with a smile

on his face. He knew that one home run would not quiet all those people who doubted that he could play. He knew it wouldn't persuade people to accept him. But it did feel good to show what he could do.

In his next at bat, he showed his versatility when he bunted for a base hit. He stole second base and advanced to third on a ground out. He took a long lead off third and so unnerved the pitcher with his quick moves that the pitcher stopped just as he was about to throw the ball to the plate. That's called a "balk," and when it happens, all the base runners are moved one base forward. Robinson trotted to home plate, scoring his second run of the day.

Robinson's heroics continued in the game. He singled and scored in the seventh. He bunted for a hit and scored again in the eighth. Montreal won the game 14–1.

His entire season was just as triumphant as his debut. His .349 batting average and his 113 runs scored were the best in the International League. He stole 40 bases, and fielded his second base position with only 10 errors in 124 games.

His performance, excellent by any standard, was even more remarkable because of the pressure he was under and the abuse he was forced to endure.

On the field at his second base position, players charged into him with spikes flying when he tried to turn a **double play**. At the plate, more often than other players, it seemed, he had to drop to the ground to get out of the way of **"brushback" pitches**. Even if he suspected that players were trying to hurt him, he shrugged it off, saying that they were just playing hard and trying to win.

At the end of the season, as winners of the International League pennant, Montreal faced Louisville, winners of the American Association pennant, in what was called the Little World Series. Louisville, Kentucky, was the most segregated city in which Robinson would play that year. The field where the first three games of the series would be played had a separate section for blacks that held less than 500 people. Though cheers from the packed black section were loud, they were drowned out by the boos of the white fans every time Robinson came to the plate. Montreal lost two of the three games and Robinson had only one hit.

Back in the friendly atmosphere of Montreal for the remaining games, Robinson exploded at the plate, driving in the winning runs in two of the games. The Royals, thanks to the season-long heroics of the first black player in organized baseball, were the Little World Series champions. The next question on everyone's mind was "Could he do as well in the major leagues?"

When he started spring training the next season, he was still on the Montreal roster. Branch Rickey, however, wanted to bring him up to the Dodgers before the season started. Rickey was afraid, however, that if he just issued an order from his office, the players would be less willing to accept him. Some of the Dodgers were from the South and were against playing with a black man.

Instead, Rickey hoped Robinson's play would be so stunning in spring training that the team would demand that Robinson be moved up to the Dodgers. Before that could happen, the situation became worse than Rickey imagined. Some of the Dodgers began passing around a petition of protest against Robinson.

Rickey called all those he suspected of taking part in the plot and told them he would not put up with a protest. The majority of the players agreed with Rickey and said they would welcome Robinson on the club. The fight for the petition died, but there was still tension among the Dodgers about the subject.

On the field, Robinson did all he could to prove he belonged on the Dodgers. In **exhibition games** against them, he pounded out hits, beat out bunts, and ran the bases with his usual abandon. Just before the Dodgers ended their spring training

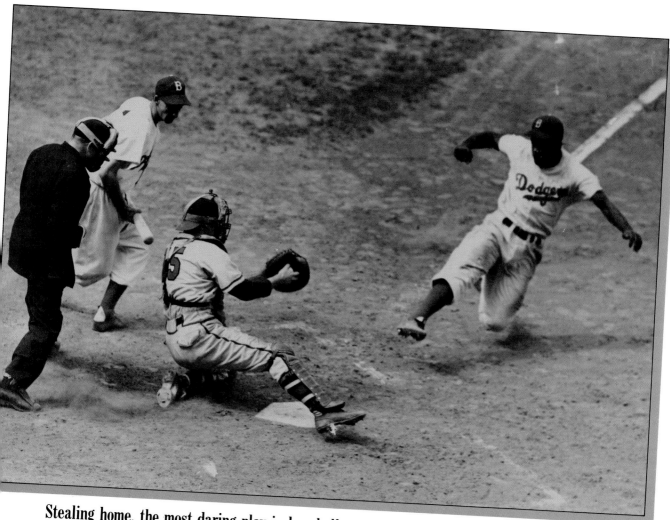

Stealing home, the most daring play in baseball, was Robinson's specialty.

schedule, Robinson was added to the Dodgers **roster**.

His major league debut didn't even draw as much attention as his appearance with Montreal had the year before. On April 15, Robinson was in the lineup as the starting first baseman, a position he had taken up in spring training. In his first four at bats, he didn't get a hit.

Through the first week of the season, he showed little of the brilliance he had displayed at Montreal or in spring training. Fans were wondering if he really did have the ability to play in the major leagues.

Then the Philadelphia Phillies, lead by manager Ben Chapman, came to town. They unleashed their flood of abuse at Robinson. They shouted comments about thick lips. They said blacks had thick skulls. They

yelled that Robinson's teammates would get diseases from sharing a locker room with him.

He heard clearly everything they said. He later wrote, "I have to admit that this day, of all the unpleasant days of my life, brought me nearer to cracking up than I have ever been. For one wild and rage-crazed minute I thought, 'To hell with Mr. Rickey's "noble experiment."' I thought what a cleansing thing it would be to let go."

Instead, showing that courage can mean choosing *not* to act, Robinson ignored the insults and turned to the plate to bat. He closed off his ears to the sounds from the Phillies dugout and concentrated on winning the game.

The taunting continued through the

game, but in the eighth inning, Robinson got his revenge. With the score tied 0–0, he singled. With the next Dodger at bat, he took off for second and advanced to third when the catcher threw the ball into centerfield. He then scored on a single, producing the only run in a 1–0 Dodger win.

Something else happened during that series with the Phillies. Robinson's teammates came to his defense. Eddie Stanky, the Dodger second baseman, shouted back at the Phillies, "You cowards! Why don't you pick on somebody who can fight back!" Even Dixie Walker, one of the players who had led the petition drive, told his friend Chapman to cut it out.

Rickey later said the actions of the Phillies unified the team, not one of whose members "was willing to sit by and see someone kick around a man who had his hands tied behind his back."

The season continued and Robinson endured more taunts and threats. Hotels accepted the rest of the team but turned him away. Pitchers purposely threw at his head when he was at bat. Players slid into him with spikes flying. But when he was knocked down, he got back up without a word. When he was called names, he didn't answer back. When he was denied admission to a hotel, he found lodging elsewhere.

Despite the enormous pressure on him, he proved by the end of the season that he deserved his place in the major leagues. He ended with a batting average of .297. He scored 125 runs, second in the league. He led the league in stolen bases with 29. *The Sporting News* named him Rookie of the Year, and he helped the Dodgers to the National League pennant.

During his ten-year career, Robinson claimed many more honors. He was named the league's Most Valuable Player in 1949 when he batted .342 to lead the league, drove in 124 runs and scored 122 runs. He was even more spectacular in the field. From his second base position, he

committed only 11 errors for a .986 fielding percentage. In 1962, he became the first black player to be voted into the Baseball Hall of Fame.

After his fabulous rookie year, no one could argue any more that blacks didn't belong in organized baseball. His example both on and off the field gave owners and fans no reason to discriminate. After his debut season, Robinson again became his fiery self and let his combativeness show.

The change in the game's color barrier was slow, but other owners signed black baseball players, and soon the sight of a black man on the field was no longer an oddity. Jackie Robinson had the courage to accept the role of the man who broke baseball's color line. He insured the success of the integration of baseball when he answered the insults of the Phillies not with his fists but with the crack of his bat.

Robinson chose to answer taunts and insults with his play on the field.

FOR THE EXTRA POINT

Adler, David A. *Jackie Robinson: He Was the First*. New York: Holiday House, 1989.

Alvarez, Mark. *The Official Baseball Hall of Fame Story of Jackie Robinson*. New York: Little Simon, 1990.

Cohen, Barbara. *Thank You, Jackie Robinson*. New York: Lothrop, 1988.

Davidson, Margaret. *The Story of Jackie Robinson: Bravest Man in Baseball*. New York: Dell, 1988.

Honig, Donald. *Baseball: When the Grass Was Real*. New York: Coward, McCann and Geoghegan, 1976. (Advanced readers.)

O'Connor, Jim. *Jackie Robinson and the Story of All-Black Baseball*. New York: Random House, 1989.

Peterson, Robert. *Only the Ball Was White*. Englewood Cliffs, N.J.: Prentice Hall, 1970. (Advanced readers.)

Robinson, Jackie, *Baseball Has Done It*. New York: Lippincott, 1964. (Advanced readers.)

Robinson, Jackie and Duckett, Alfred. *I Never Had It Made*. New York: Fawcett, Crest, 1974. (Advanced readers.)

Rust, Art, Jr. *"Get That Nigger Off the Field!"*. New York: Delacorte, 1976. (Advanced readers.)

Tygiel, Jules. *Baseball's Great Experiment: Jackie Robinson and His Legacy*. New York: Random House, 1983. (Advanced readers.)

JACK ROOSEVELT ROBINSON

CAREER STATISTICS

Minor Leagues

Year	Team	Pos.	Games	AB	R	H	HR	RBI	BA
1946	Montreal	2B	124	444	113	155	3	66	.349

Major Leagues

Year	Team	Pos.	Games	AB	R	H	HR	RBI	BA
1947	Brooklyn	IB	151	590	125	175	12	48	.297
1948	Brooklyn	INF	147	574	108	170	12	85	.296
1949	Brooklyn	2B	156	593	122	203	16	124	.342
1950	Brooklyn	2B	144	518	99	170	14	81	.328
1951	Brooklyn	2B	153	548	106	185	19	88	.338
1952	Brooklyn	2B	149	510	104	157	19	75	.308
1953	Brooklyn	INF-OF	136	484	109	159	12	95	.329
1954	Brooklyn	INF-OF	124	386	62	120	15	59	.311
1955	Brooklyn	INF-OF	105	317	51	81	8	36	.256
1956	Brooklyn	INF-OF	117	357	61	98	10	43	.275
Major League Totals			1382	4877	947	1518	137	734	.311

Pos. = Position   R = Runs   H = Hits   RBI = Runs Batted In   BA = Batting Average
AB = At Bats   2B = Second Base   HR = Home Runs   1B = First Base   INF = Infield   OF = Outfield

After Riddles crossed the finish line in Nome,
she shared the victory with her dogs.

LIBBY RIDDLES

Braving the Cold

Libby Riddles had a decision to make. She was leading the 1985 Iditarod Trail Sled Dog Race after fifteen days and had just arrived at the *checkpoint* in Shaktoolik, Alaska, with her dog team. A fierce blizzard was blowing and had been for the last 20 miles into Shaktoolik. Gusts ranged from 40 to 60 miles per hour. The next checkpoint was 58 miles away. The first 10 or 15 of those miles was flat marshland, then the trail moved across frozen sea until Koyuk.

The storm showed no signs of letting up. If she set off for Koyuk, the wind would be blowing against her the whole way. Visibility was so bad that she might not be able to see the stakes that marked the trail, and therefore, she took the chance of getting lost. Going out in such a blizzard could be very dangerous, even deadly.

But if Riddles stayed in Shaktoolik until the weather improved, the competitors behind her would catch up. She had worked so hard to get the lead. Those efforts would have been in vain if she stayed at the checkpoint. Her dogs were in good shape after traveling the 908 miles from Anchorage, but she knew they were not fast enough to keep up with the other teams for the final 229 miles to Nome if they all left Shaktoolik at the same time. The other drivers would be pulling into the checkpoint soon. She had to decide quickly. Should she stay or should she go?

The Iditarod Trail Sled Dog Race is the most famous long-distance sled dog race in the world. It covers some 1,200 miles between Anchorage, which is in the southeast part of Alaska, to Nome, which is in the north central part of the state on the Seward Peninsula.

Before airplanes and highways became

common forms of travel in Alaska, sled dog teams performed tasks like delivering mail and supplies to towns in the region. In remote areas of the state, a dog sled is still a useful way to travel in winter. Sled dog racing has been around since the early part of the century when the different mining camps in the area challenged each other to races.

The first Iditarod race was held in 1973, one year after Riddles moved to the state at age sixteen. She was born in 1957 and grew up in St. Cloud, Minnesota, the daughter of a college professor. Seeking a more adventurous life, she rushed to finish high school in 2½ years and then moved to Alaska. Soon, she began raising and training dogs for sled dog racing.

The dogs used for racing are a mix of three main breeds—the malamute, the Siberian husky, and the generic husky. The malamute is a large dog, weighing up to 100 pounds, with a heavy coat. The Siberian husky is a smaller breed with a coat of light gray and dark gray. The generic husky is not a specific breed, but a mix of its own, drawn from village work dogs and other dogs that lived in the north.

Racing dogs must have stamina to travel the long distances required and speed to move the sled quickly over flat areas of the trail. Most sled dogs average forty to fifty pounds and trot at a speed of 10 to 15 miles per hour.

Riddles eventually settled in Teller, which is on the Seward Peninsula, just over 100 miles from the Soviet Union. She first entered the Iditarod in 1980 and finished 18th. In 1981, she entered again and finished 20th. When the 1985 Iditarod came around, no one expected much of her. She was using virtually the same dog team that her partner, Joe Garnie, had used the year before when he finished third, but most of the 63 other **"mushers,"** or dog sled drivers, didn't give her much of a chance. They didn't think she had enough experience.

Riddles knew she had a good team, and with a little luck and some sound strategy, she might become the first woman to win the race. She wasn't going to go out fast at first. Some mushers tried to put as much distance as they could between themselves and the pack of teams early in the race and then hoped that lead was big enough to keep anyone from catching them. Others just tried to stay within a few hours of the leader, conserving their dogs' energy until the final few hundred miles, when they dashed for Nome and passed the sleds ahead of them. Riddles adopted the latter strategy, trying not to tire her dogs out before the last part of the race.

On March 2, 1985, Riddles and her team of fifteen dogs lined up on Fourth Avenue in Anchorage to await the start of the race. The race officials came by with paint and put a small purple spot on each of her dogs' heads to make sure she wouldn't change dogs during the race.

The sleds were started two minutes apart, beginning at 9 A.M. The countdown for her time began.

Three...two...one...Go! The dogs began to move, pulling their **harnesses** tight. The sled slid along the snow on Fourth Avenue, and the crowds applauded. The race was under way!

The first stretch was 20 miles along the Anchorage city race trail and a power-line trail to Eagle River. Running through a small area of trees, the dogs became tangled and Riddles had to stop to work them loose. Otherwise, her team was energetic and fast, reaching speeds of 20 miles per hour. Later, during a rocky passage, one of the mushers flipped and broke his collarbone. Riddles had a bumpy ride but made it through the same part without incident. The day would get worse for her.

Once at Eagle River, all the teams were transported by truck to Settlers Bay, where the next leg was started that same day. The next stop was Knik, only 8 miles away.

Before then her dogs became so badly knotted in a grove of trees that one of them almost choked. She freed them again and was on her way.

The next segment contained some tricky turns down steep hills, and Riddles was riding her foot brake pretty hard. Around one corner, she noticed that the brake wasn't catching as well as it had been. The sled hardly slowed at all. When she looked down to see what was the matter, she saw that it had broken. She was able to get a replacement in Knik. If it had broken past that stop, she would have had to return to Knik to find one. Riddles arrived in Knik at 4:31 P.M. in 32nd place. She spent no more than half an hour fixing the brake before continuing on to the next stop at Rabbit Lake, 52 miles away.

About 25 miles out of Knik, she decided to rest her dogs and give them a snack. She tied the team to a small tree near the trail. As they were stopped, some other teams passed and the dogs became anxious to follow. They pulled forward, bending the tree and pulling tight the knot Riddles had tied. She couldn't undo the knot and she didn't want to cut the rope, so she began to chop at the tree with her axe. When the tree finally gave way, the dogs took off, and all Riddles could do was grab onto the tree. The dogs pulled her face down through the snow until she couldn't hold any longer. They disappeared into the darkness of the night. It looked as if the race was lost before it had really begun.

She walked along the trail, hoping to catch up with them when she noticed a light behind her. It was another musher. She explained what had happened and he gave her a ride. Half an hour later, they found the dogs, resting in the snow. Another musher had tied them to a tree to keep them from getting away. Shaken but still happy to find her dogs, she continued on to Rabbit Lake, reaching the checkpoint at 1:10 in the morning in 17th place.

Susan Butcher, one of the few other

TRAIL TALK

checkpoint: a place along the trail of a dog-sled race where drivers stop to feed and rest their dogs and themselves and where race officials register the racers' time and position.

frostbite: an injury in which parts of the body are exposed to intense cold, damaging tissues in that part.

harness: the straps and bindings that hold a dog in the team and allow it to pull the sled.

headlamp: a light that the dog-sled drivers wear on a strap around their head to help them see the trail at night.

mushers: dog-sled drivers, so called because the term "mush" was a word the drivers used to urge on their dogs, possibly from the French word *marcher*, meaning "go."

runner: one of the strips of metal or wood on which the sled rests and which allow it to move smoothly over ice and through snow.

trot: a running speed at which a dog (or other animal) moves by lifting alternating diagonal pairs of legs.

wheel dog: the dog closest to the sled; it pulls the greatest load.

---

women in the race and twice before a second-place finisher, was leading the race at Rabbit Lake but had experienced even more trouble than Riddles. The deep snow in the area had driven moose onto the race trail, which, since the snow was packed, provided easier walking. Near the Sustina River, a moose had become tangled in Butcher's team, trampling two of her dogs to death. Another musher, who was carrying a gun for just such an emergency, shot the moose and prevented further injury to Butcher's dogs, or possibly to Butcher herself. Butcher dropped out of the race.

The Rabbit Lake checkpoint had dog food

that the racers had sent ahead in marked bags before the race. Riddles set up and lit the portable stove she carried with her, filled a pan with water from a hole in the lake ice, and heated some chopped-up frozen meat from her bag. She gave the dogs one serving, which they ate heartily, and put another serving in an insulated container for a meal down the trail between checkpoints. She repeated the procedure at each checkpoint. Then she examined the paws of the dogs for cuts. At 4:00 A.M., two hours and fifty minutes after she stopped, she was back on the trail again.

Skwentna lay 34 miles away. Riddles and her team made good time over the small

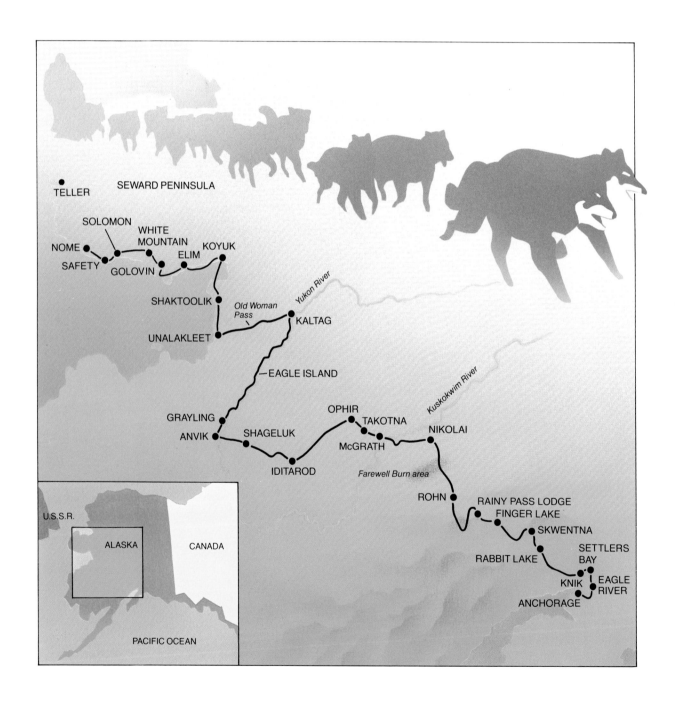

hills, but at one point a moose blocked the trail. She directed her team in a wide arc around the creature, and the dogs kept their attention on the trail. She made it past safely and reached Skwentna at 9:30 A.M.

The next section followed the ice on the frozen Skwentna River before moving into the foothills of the Alaska Range. Mount McKinley, the highest peak in North America at 20,320 feet, is part of that range.

Deep snow covered the next 45 miles to Finger Lake, and the trail hadn't been packed down yet. The going was tough for the dogs, and she had to stop and put special dog boots on their feet to keep them from getting snow between their foot pads. By the time she reached Finger Lake at 2:10 in the morning, Riddles was tired. Her team was 19th into the checkpoint, and she was within three hours of the leader. She would try to keep that close until late in the race when she could make her push to the front.

She cooked up another meal for the dogs and had some soup herself. She was able to hang up some clothes to dry in the checkpoint cabin, but the cabin was crowded with mushers and she returned to her sled outside to catch some sleep before moving on. The next day's travel would cover a treacherous descent into the Happy River canyon, a drop of more than 500 feet. The trail at the Happy River canyon zigzagged down the steep drop. The drivers had to make several sharp turns at high speeds.

Riddles left Finger Lake shortly after 8 A.M. The temperature early that day was −16 degrees but would later warm up to 18 degrees. When she reached the canyon, she noticed the tracks of several drivers ahead of her who had already crashed. She started her team down slowly, but they picked up speed and were soon racing down the hill. One of the **runners** of her sled hit a deep dent in the snow, and the sled turned upside down. Riddles held tight and yelled, "Stay!" Her dogs halted as Riddles righted herself.

She looked at the damage. The snow hook she used to anchor the sled whenever she stopped had torn her jacket and had also hit her hand, causing a knuckle to swell. She put some snow on the knuckle to relieve the swelling. By the time she reached the next checkpoint at Rainy Pass, storm clouds were gathering over the mountains.

Riddles learned at Rainy Pass that, because of the snow, airplanes had not been able to fly ahead to drop dog food at the next two checkpoints. The competitors had to wait there until the weather cleared.

Three days later, the mushers got the word that they could head out. The next checkpoint was Rohn Roadhouse, 88 miles away. Riddles was well rested for a change, but so were all of the others.

The fresh snow made it hard for the dogs to get solid footing, and that made for slow progress. However, the weather was clear and the temperature went as high as a comfortable 21 degrees Fahrenheit. The wind occasionally blew the loose snow across the tracks of the teams ahead, making it difficult to find the trail. Riddles's lead dog, Dugan, was good at sniffing out the scent of the dogs that had gone before, so Riddles let him do most of the navigating.

The trail went through a high ridge called Ptarmigan Pass and wound down into a narrow river canyon called Hell's Gate. Along the way, Riddles and her team had some of the most pleasant traveling of the race. She described it in her book *Race across Alaska*: "The site was picture-book Alaska: regal spruce lining the river, mountains all around, fresh snow. Then add what has to be the freshest air in the world, crisp and fragrant and invigorating."

After nearly fifteen hours on the trail, Riddles arrived at Rohn Roadhouse at 2 A.M. As usual, she cooked for the dogs first. She hung the dog boots near the fire to dry and dug out some food for herself among her frozen supplies.

She remained well back in 18th place but was still only three hours behind the leader because of the delay at Rainy Pass. After an eleven-hour stop at Rohn, she hitched up her team and set out for Nikolai. The trails alternated between meadows and woods, and Riddles found the going easy. Every once in a while she would stop to feed the dogs a snack of frozen whitefish. Then it was back to work.

The Iditarod route took the mushers through an area of 362,000 acres called the Farewell Burn, where a forest fire, the largest in the history of Alaska, had raged for two months in 1977. At the time of year the race was held, it was covered with snow. After Farewell Burn, the trail was easy enough to follow that she could slip a cassette in her Walkman and listen to Bob Marley and the Wailers.

As night fell, the snow became heavier and the light from the headlamp she wore gave little clue to the direction of the trail. The dogs were making good time, however, and she caught a few of the teams ahead of her, so she knew she was going the right way.

By the time she reached the village of Nikolai, she had gained ten places on the leader but had lost thirty minutes. That was OK. Nome was still a long distance away.

The next segment to McGrath was a short one, only 48 miles. The day was clear, but because of the new snow and the warm weather (33 degrees), the dogs tired easily and needed frequent rest stops. Off the trail, a musher would sink into the snow up to the waist. Riddles covered the distance in nine hours and fifty minutes.

After getting only an hour of sleep, Riddles was on the back of her sled again heading for the next stop at Ophir. The temperature rose to 37 degrees, and the melting snow began to stick to the sled's runners, making the dogs work twice as hard. While she was resting the dogs, Riddles saw a few teams pass her. She was most concerned with the team of Rick Swenson, whose dogs still looked very fresh

and fast. Riddles didn't dare chase them at that point. It was hard to let them go by, but her dogs were tired and needed a slower pace.

When she finally arrived in Ophir, she found out that the race had been stopped once again because of the snow ahead. The race manager said it was "by far the worst weather" in the history of the race. Instead of the mass start after the race was delayed at Rainy Pass, at Ophir the teams were released in the order which they arrived. All the mushers agreed this would be fairer.

When the race started again, Riddles left Ophir at 11:16 P.M. on the way to Iditarod, the town that gave the race its name. In the early twentieth century, during the Alaska gold rush, it had been a town of several thousand people. Now it was just a ghost town with a few abandoned buildings. The trail opened up after Ophir, with fewer trees and more flat stretches of land. Riddles still took it easy on her team, resting them often. But after the checkpoint at Iditarod, she knew the real race would begin. All the teams were rested because of the two weather stops. The competition would really heat up.

Riddles arrived in Iditarod in 4th place. The two leaders, Tim Osmar and Burt Bomhoff, had driven their teams hard over the last stretch to the checkpoint in pursuit of the $2,000 cash prize for the first musher to reach Iditarod. Riddles thought, therefore, that only one other team would be as fresh as hers when they left the checkpoint.

She fed her dogs and got out of there as quickly as she could. Two other sleds left with her. They were three and a half hours behind the leader. By the time they left, eleven other teams had pulled into the checkpoint, so they didn't have much of a headstart. Besides that, the snow had started up again and the temperatures were around freezing, so the going was slow.

The trail was covered with the wet snow. Sometime in the night the three sleds caught and passed the leader, who had stopped for a rest. Those three took turns breaking the trail. During her turn, Riddles hated the extra work it took to plow through the fresh snow. Then she thought about her position. She wrote in *Race across Alaska*: "I was miserable and feeling sorry for myself, when I suddenly realized that...for the first time ever, I was leading the Iditarod race. I was in first place. First place."

Later in the night, the four teams stopped to sleep, and, figuring they had such a large lead, didn't even bother to move out of the trail. They awakened to the sound of Rick Swenson's voice telling them to get out of the way. Behind him were ten or more drivers. Their lead had been eliminated.

The 90 miles between Iditarod and Anvik were a roller coaster of hills. Then the land

Riddles cut her nose after a mishap with her headlamp, but she continued down the trail.

flattened out as the trail ran on top of the frozen Innoko River. Through other nights of travel, Riddles had been able to doze occasionally on the back of the sled. She tried to fight off sleep now. The trail turned away from the river into a forest. With all those trees around, she should stay awake. Still, she couldn't help herself. She was too tired.

Her sleep was interrupted by the WHACK of a low-hanging branch hitting her in the head. It knocked her **headlamp** down onto her nose, hard. It also snuffed out the light. She was in darkness. She put her hand to her nose and felt the blood streaming from it. She was, however, more concerned about the headlamp. She switched it on. It worked! Then she found a tissue for her nose.

Riddles's team trotted into Anvik at a quarter after one in the morning. She lingered there just under five hours, feeding the dogs a hot meal and catching a couple of hours of sleep herself. Several teams passed her while she slept, and when she arrived in Grayling, 18 miles north on the frozen Yukon River, she had slipped back to 14th place. In Grayling, she waited out the heat of the day and left at 2:50 P.M. She was in 7th place as she left. She was encouraged by the way the dogs looked. With the temperature dropping rapidly, the snow was becoming harder, so she stopped often to put the boots on the dogs. Stewpot, **the wheel dog**, or the one closest to the sled, was laboring in the early afternoon but looked more energetic as the temperature fell.

The dogs didn't mind the cold, but at −40 degrees the temperature was getting uncomfortable for Riddles. As the trail followed the Yukon River, she had to be careful to avoid **frostbite**. She kept moving her toes to keep the circulation going. She stood on one runner of the sled and pushed along the ground with the other foot. Then she would switch to the second runner and move the other foot.

The other mushers ahead of her stopped for food, but she'd been stopping too much, so she decided to forge ahead. She was all alone in front. When she reached Eagle Island checkpoint at 5 A.M., everyone in the cabin was asleep. In *Race across Alaska*, she wrote, "Someone said he was amazed the first musher was a 'girl.'"

Thirteen days into the race and she was in first place. It was 435 miles to Nome. Nobody had given her much of a chance at the start, but two-thirds of the way through the race, she was leading.

The weather stayed cold, but the trail left the Yukon River at Kaltag, 70 miles from Eagle Island. Off the river, the weather warmed up. Riddles and a group of four other sleds were setting the pace. Any of them was within striking distance of the lead.

The next stretch was a 90-mile section that was originally a trade route for Eskimos and Indians from the inland villages to the coast of the Bering Sea at the town of Unalakleet. Miles outside of Unalakleet, Riddles saw wolf tracks in the snow. Closer in, snowmobile tracks made it difficult to find the trail, and one machine burst out of the darkness, almost hitting her team.

Lavon Barve arrived in the town just fifteen minutes ahead of Riddles at 11:41, but in the morning at 6:00 when he wanted to leave, he decided his dogs weren't ready and headed back to bed. Riddles was the first out of the checkpoint at 7:15 A.M. She had to drop one of her dogs at Unalakleet because of the pounding its feet had taken. The rest of the team, however, was healthy and ready to move on.

The next 40 miles to Shaktoolik were ones that Riddles knew well. She had worked in the town in 1981 as a fish buyer. As she headed north over the mountain ridges, she could see the Bering Sea off to her left. The hills were hard on the dogs, but they made good progress. With her early start, she knew it was the time to try to put some distance between her team and the others.

Closer to Shaktoolik, the weather began to worsen. A storm had moved in over the ice in Norton Sound, the next segment of the race. Riddles had opened up nearly a three-hour lead on the next musher, and she didn't want to lose it. In Shaktoolik, the storm became a blizzard. The wind was brutal. She couldn't imagine how cold it might be out there.

After feeding the dogs, she prepared to go, though she hadn't decided for sure if she would brave the weather. The 2nd-place sled came in. He saw her getting ready and told her it was "impossible." The word hit her like a avalanche. She wouldn't let anyone tell her what was impossible! She would go!

In *Race across Alaska*, she wrote: "I allowed only one thought: to keep my lead at all costs, taking it inch by inch if necessary. Winning the Iditarod was the dream that had driven me since I first raced...My goal was attainable now, and so long as I was capable of putting one foot in front of the other, no storm was going to prevent me from achieving it."

She put boots on all the dogs' feet and moved off into the teeth of the blizzard at 5:30 in the afternoon. All she could see before her was a blanket of white. The stakes marking the trail were about 100 feet apart, but visibility was much less than that. Riddles repeatedly had to stop the sled and walk ahead to find the next stake. With every stop, she stooped down and wiped snow from the faces of the dogs.

The danger of the weather and the location grew. Frostbite was a very real possibility. Because she was moving toward the bay ice, if she lost the trail, she might fall into a section of open water. That could be fatal. Visibility was worse with her goggles, so her eyes were exposed to the blasts of the wind and the whipping snow.

Three hours after leaving Shaktoolik, daylight vanished. Seeing anything was out of the question. She had to camp for the

Riddles set out from Anchorage with one goal—to become the first woman to win the Iditarod.

night. The temperature was dropping. She had to take every precaution against the cold. Protected momentarily by the sled, she struggled out of her snowdampened clothes piece by piece and squeezed into her sleeping bag. It was so cold she could only expose her fingers for a few seconds at a time to work the zipper on the sleeping bag. The dogs dug little beds in the snow and curled up in them. Their heavy coats and the insulation from the snow protected them. They all went to sleep as the storm howled around them.

The storm lightened somewhat by morning, but Riddles didn't want to spend another night on the ice. She had to move quickly.

As her team moved out onto frozen Norton Sound, Riddles moved her veteran dog Sister into the lead with Dugan. The ice was slick and the team was traveling fast. Then Riddles lost track of the trail markers. Sister and Dugan **trotted** on as if they knew exactly where they were going. Riddles let them go and trusted their instincts. Finally she saw another marker. The dogs had taken her in the right direction.

Soon, she saw the buildings of the village of Koyuk in the distance. The team trotted into the checkpoint. She had nearly a seven-hour lead on the next musher. All the other teams had stayed in Shaktoolik for the night. Her gamble had worked! All she had to do was hold on to that lead for the 200 miles into Nome, and she would be the first woman to win the Iditarod.

She kept a five-hour lead through three more checkpoints. The last checkpoint before Nome was Safety Roadhouse, just 22 miles from the finish. Sometime in the night, because of the darkness and poor markers, Riddles wandered from the trail and ended up at Solomon, several miles from the Safety checkpoint.

She stopped at a cabin, and a man directed her back to the trail. Duane Halverson was able to make up about three hours on her because of her mistake, but it was not enough.

As she encouraged the dogs on that final run to Nome, the reality of what she had accomplished hit her. Tears streamed from her eyes. Crowds lined Front Street in Nome to cheer her home. The temperature was 18 degrees but she felt warm.

FOR THE EXTRA POINT

Riddles, Libby and Jones, Tim. *Race across Alaska*. Harrisburg, Pa.: Stackpole Books, 1988. (Advanced readers.)

LIBBY RIDDLES

1985 IDITAROD PERFORMANCE

Date (March)	Checkpoint	Miles from Start	Pos.	Time In	Out
2	Knik	62	32	4:31 P.M.	5:00 P.M.
3	Rabbit Lake	114	17	1:10 A.M.	4.00 A.M.
3	Skwentna	148	17	9:31 A.M.	4:00 P.M.
4	Finger Lake	193	19	2:10 A.M.	8:05 A.M.
4–7	Rainy Pass	223	19	3:15 P.M. (March 4)	11:19 A.M. (March 7)
7	Rohn Roadhouse	271	18	2:06 A.M.	7:30 A.M.
8	Nikolai	341	8	1:26 A.M.	8:45 A.M.
9–10	McGrath	389	10	6:35 P.M. (March 9)	2:00 A.M. (March 10)
10	Takotna	412	6	4:50 A.M.	6:45 A.M.
10–11	Ophir	450	14	11:06 A.M. (March 10)	11:16 P.M. (March 11)
12	Iditarod	540	4	2:53 P.M.	8:00 P.M.
13	Shageluk	605	6	4:00 P.M.	8:15 P.M.
14	Anvik	630	14	1:16 A.M.	6:02 A.M.
14	Grayling	648	14	9:05 A.M.	2:50 P.M.
15	Eagle Island	708	1	5:00 A.M.	5:50 P.M.
16	Kaltag	778	3	3:15 A.M.	10:55 A.M.
16–17	Unalakleet	868	2	11:56 P.M. (March 16)	7:15 A.M. (March 17)
17	Shaktoolik	908	1	2:17 P.M.	5:30 P.M.
18	Koyuk	966	1	5:13 P.M.	10:16 P.M.
19	Elim	1014	1	5:45 A.M.	7:45 A.M.
19	Golovin	1042	1	12 noon	12:37 P.M.
19	White Mountain	1060	1	3:05 P.M.	7:15 P.M.
20	Safety	1115	1	4:33 A.M.	6:30 A.M.
20	Nome	1137	1	9:20 A.M.	

Riddles's Winning Time: 18 days, 0 hours, 20 minutes

Pos. = Position

King's aggressive style helped her win many tennis battles both on and off the court.

BILLIE JEAN KING

Tennis's Woman Warrior

Billie Jean King never backed down from a challenge.

In 1967, Billie Jean King defeated Ann Jones to win the women's singles title at the U.S. National Tennis Championships for the first time. Earlier that same summer, she had won the women's singles championship at Wimbledon. She was ranked No. 1 in the world for the second straight year. Ever since she started playing tennis, she had wanted to be the best. Now she should have been happy. She wasn't.

What troubled her, even from her position at the top of the rankings, was the way tennis was run. As she once said, "If you're Number One and still complaining, I felt, maybe people will realize that something really is wrong." She was disturbed by the way money was distributed in tennis. She was more disturbed by the way women players were treated. So she spoke out. And finally when words weren't enough, she acted.

In challenging the unfairness of tennis's ruling organizations, she showed the same passionate determination that marked her play on the court. She risked her career by criticizing the organizations. She struggled to organize the women into their own tour. Finally, she played one match that determined the respectability of women's tennis.

When Billie Jean Moffitt (King is her married name) was growing up in Long Beach, California, in the 1940s and early 1950s, she loved all sports. She played basketball, softball, and even football with the other kids in the neighborhood.

Her mother, Betty, wasn't too keen on the idea of her daughter playing a rough sport like football, so she asked Billie Jean if she would consider taking up a sport that was

NET TALK

backhand: a stroke during which the player strikes the ball by swinging the racket forward starting on the side of the body opposite the hand holding the racket.

default: a match ended before its normal completion because one player, by injury or other reasons, can't continue to play.

double-fault: two consecutive unsuccessful serves; that is, when the ball does not land in the opponent's service area after two attempts; the player receiving the serve wins the point.

drop shot: a stroke in which a player hits the ball with strong backspin so that it will bounce very low on the other side of the net and very close to the net.

forehand: a stroke during which the player strikes the ball by swinging the racket forward on the same side of the body as the hand that holds the racket, as if hitting the ball with the palm of the hand.

lob: a shot hit very high so the ball will land close to the opponent's baseline; usually intended to travel over the head of an opponent who has moved close to the net.

mixed doubles: tennis played with two-person teams, where one teammate is male and one female.

rally: any exchange of shots after the ball has been put into play by a serve.

serve: the stroke by which a player starts a game by hitting the ball into the opponent's service court.

service toss: throwing the ball into the air in preparation for striking the ball during a serve.

set: a group of games which a player wins by being the first to reach six by a margin of two.

more "ladylike." Billie Jean asked her father, Bill, which sport would fit that description, and after thinking about it for a while, he suggested tennis.

Billie Jean wasn't quite sure how to play tennis, but if her parents approved, she was willing to give it a try. The only problem was equipment. The Moffits weren't rich—Bill was a fireman—and rackets were expensive. She began doing odd jobs around the neighborhood to earn enough money for one. Finally she had enough to buy one but didn't know how to play.

At age eleven she began taking lessons at the public courts in the city. Soon, Billie Jean became obsessed with the game and began playing every day. Even then she sensed that tennis was the sport for her. She was big and stocky for her age, 5′4″ and 125 pounds, and she soon developed strong,

powerful strokes.

In her first age-group tournament, she discovered that boys and girls were not treated equally. Her mother had made her a pair of shorts to play in, but when the director of the tournament saw that she was not in a dress, he wouldn't let her pose in the photograph of the competitors.

She won a few matches in age-group tournaments the next year and kept improving. By 1958 she was ranked highly in Southern California for ages fifteen and under.

Billie Jean was also developing a driving ambition that would be satisfied with nothing less than perfection. The pastor of her church was Bob Richards, a pole vaulter who won Olympic gold medals in that event in 1952 and 1956. He asked Billie Jean what she wanted to be when she grew up. Her response to that innocent question was, "I'm going to be the best tennis player in the world."

She began traveling to more tournaments and soon had acquired a No. 5 national ranking among girls fifteen and under and was a regular on the junior circuit.

The next two years—1959 and 1960—were taken up with travel and tennis. She and some of the other girls from Southern California played in the best junior tournaments on the East Coast. Billie Jean's parents were paying for part of the trip, but most of the money came from a group called the Long Beach Tennis Patrons, which was formed especially to give promising tennis players who couldn't afford to travel the opportunity to play in the best tournaments around the country.

Sharpening her aggressive game against some of the best competition in the country helped Billie Jean, at age seventeen, achieve a No. 4 ranking among all U.S. women. And she was still in high school!

In fact, just two days before she was scheduled to graduate from Long Beach Polytechnic High, she left for Wimbledon, England, to play in the All England Lawn Tennis Championships, the most prestigious tennis tournament in the world.

At her first Wimbledon, she lost in the first round of the singles and teamed with a fellow Southern California teenager named Karen Hantze to compete in the doubles. Everyone was surprised when Billie Jean and her partner won the doubles.

She returned home to find that she and Hantze had been named to the U.S. Wightman Cup team. Every year the United States and Great Britain held a competition between their best women tennis players called the Wightman Cup. Opposing the American girls for the British team were the 1961 Wimbledon singles champion and that same year's Wimbledon runner-up. Play was a combination of both doubles and singles matches.

She and her teammates pulled off one of the greatest upsets in Wightman Cup history by defeating the heavily favored English women.

After the Wightman Cup, which was held in Chicago, Billie Jean returned home. Today in the same situation, Billie Jean would be sought after by colleges with tennis scholarships to offer. She could use her athletic ability, as thousands of young women do now, to pay for her college education. Or, since she had proved herself to be one of the best women players in the world, she could turn professional and play for tournament prize money.

But in 1961 none of those options existed for a good woman tennis player, and Billie Jean did what hundreds of girls before her had done: She put away her tennis racket and went to college.

Enrolling in Los Angeles State College, she lived the life of an ordinary college student, living at home and working at a part-time job to make ends meet. In the spring she would take out her racket and

TENNIS COURT SURFACES

clay: a loose, almost sandy surface that causes slower play. The ball bounces higher, allowing players to reach balls more easily. Players who stay on the baseline generally have more success on clay. The French Open is played on a surface of red clay.

grass: closely cropped grass provides a fast surface on which the ball skids more easily, favoring players who hit the ball hard especially during their serves. The All-England Championship at Wimbledon is the most famous grass court tournament.

hardcourt: a name for courts which have a concrete base and usually some kind of rubberized coating. These courts play faster than clay but slower than grass. They provide the best footing of the three. The U.S. Open is played on a hardcourt surface.

play a few tournaments to get her form back. Then she would make the trip to Wimbledon and continue through the summer playing in grass-court tournaments in the United States. She advanced to the finals at Wimbledon in 1963 and the semifinals in 1964, even though in effect she was only a part-time tennis player. She continued to play in Wightman Cup matches and she held on to her national ranking, but she wasn't getting any better.

In the summer of 1964, she was finally forced to make a decision. Should she commit all her time to tennis and try to become the best in the world, or should she give it up and opt for some other career? Or should she just settle down and get married? A rich Australian tennis fan had seen Billie Jean play and thought she should develop her talent more fully. He offered to bring her to Australia for a few months to train with the great Australian tennis player Mervyn Rose.

Her decision was complicated by the fact that at school she had met a player for the men's tennis team named Larry King. They had been dating for two years, and she didn't want to be apart from him in Australia for those few months. He encouraged her to take advantage of the opportunity anyway, and three weeks before she left, they were engaged.

She returned from Australia with a complete, improved game. She had worked to eliminate her weaknesses. She changed her **service toss** to get more power out of her **serve**. She shortened the backswing on her **forehand** for more control.

It took her some time to get used to her new game, but when she did, she started enjoying success she never had achieved before. She made it to the finals of the U.S. National Championships in 1965 and the semifinals of Wimbledon that same year. After the tennis season, she and Larry were married, and she changed her name to Billie Jean King.

As hard as it is for us to believe now, in spite of King's success on the court, she and Larry still needed the $32 a week she made as a tennis instructor. There was no such thing as professional tennis for women, and the best tournaments—the U.S. and French national championships and Wimbledon—were open only to amateurs. Players like King received some financial help from the U.S. Lawn Tennis Association (USLTA), which is now called simply the U.S. Tennis Association, and from private sponsors, like the Australian man who helped her.

Larry was working in a factory at nights while finishing his studies, and he hoped to enroll in law school before long. In spite of their economic hardships, Billie Jean continued her quest to be the best tennis player in the world. In her mind, to reach that goal meant one thing: winning at Wimbledon.

In 1966 she reached the finals against a player from Brazil named Maria Bueno. She kept Bueno off-balance with deep serves, behind which King would rush to the net. When Bueno came to the net herself, King **lobbed** over her head. By the third set, Billie Jean was in complete control and lost only one game in that **set** to win 6–3, 3–6, 6–1. She described the feeling in her autobiography *Billie Jean*: "On match point I threw my racket in the air, and I was suddenly as happy as I'd ever been in my life. Finally, I was Number One. In my mind I was the best player in the world."

Ascending to that height gave her a forum for speaking out about the game. She saw many things wrong with the way tennis was organized at its highest levels, and she expressed her opinions in press conferences and interviews. The thing that angered her most was that tennis officials tried to preserve the idea of top-ranked players being amateurs. An "amateur" is a player who doesn't take money for participating in a sport.

There was no prize money for events like the U.S. Nationals, but the top players were given money to appear in the tournament and officials called the money "expenses." This seemed underhanded to King, and she wanted to bring it all out in the open. So she talked about it to the press. The scrappy kid from the concrete courts of Long Beach began to irritate the wealthy men from country clubs who ran the sport. In 1967, after a press conference at the U.S. Nationals, the president of the USLTA decided to have a talk with her. He warned her to soften her criticism or the organization would suspend her. Her reply to him was defiant. "Look at the game," she said to him. "Things are so bad I'm not sure I even want to keep playing unless something changes." The president didn't suspend her, and she went on to win the singles title at the tournament.

Other players began to follow King's brave example. They too spoke of the under-the-table payments and argued for prize money awards. Finally, the tennis organizations in the U.S. and around the world began to break down. They couldn't suspend everyone who spoke out, because people wanted to see those players, especially the top ones like King. Finally, in October of 1967, the British Lawn Tennis Association voted to have "open" tennis, which allowed amateurs and professionals to compete together. The other organizations soon followed. The U.S. National Championships became the U.S. Open, as it is known today.

During this time of turmoil in tennis, King became the most dominant women's player in the world. She won three Wimbledon titles from 1966 to 1968, won the U.S. Nationals in 1967, and captured the Australian championship in 1968. In 1967 she was named Athlete of the Year by the Associated Press.

While King was happy that players who devoted their lives to their sport were finally being paid for the time they put in, she was still upset by the differences in the treatment of male and female professionals. In the first open tournament, the British

Hard Court Championships in 1968, the first-place prize for men's singles was $2,400. The winner of the women's singles title received only $720.

After winning the first open Wimbledon in 1968, King suffered from a sore knee, which eventually required surgery. She missed much of the 1969 tennis season while it healed. And when she came back from that injury in 1970 she found she had the same problem with the other knee, which also required surgery.

King still attended the tournaments when she was recovering and began hearing the complaints of other women about the inequality of the prize money. Two years after the era of open tennis began, King won the Italian Open and received a winner's check for $600. The men's champion received $3,500. The men were getting paid nearly six times what the women were earning. That ratio held true for other tournaments as well.

To King, this seemed terribly unfair. This time she had to do more than simply speak out. Criticism wasn't enough. She had to act.

She and some of the other players decided to organize a tournament themselves. They convinced Virginia Slims cigarettes to put up the prize money, and nine women players agreed to skip one of the USLTA's scheduled events to participate in the new event. For defying the USLTA, the organization briefly suspended the Americans who played in the tournament. Since the USLTA controlled events like the U.S. Nationals, the U.S. Clay Court Championships, and other important U.S. tournaments, the women knew that if they continued on their own, they could be giving up the chance to play in those tournaments.

Along with King, three other players (Rosie Casals, Frankie Durr, and Ann Jones) began to organize more events. By January of 1971, a Virginia Slims tour was formed, with fourteen tournaments in the

King and Rosie Casals won the doubles at Wimbledon in 1971 and started a women's tour that same year.

winter and spring of that year and fifteen scheduled for the following fall. A minimum of $10,000 total prize money was offered for each event.

Not everyone had the courage to break with the USLTA. King described the feelings she and her fellow players had about that first tour in her 1974 autobiography: "A majority of the women were still reluctant [to join the new tour], however. They thought we would fail and they didn't want to risk being a part of that failure...It was kind of scary. We felt like we were alone, and there were a lot of times when I had my doubts; but deep down I think I always felt we'd make it—at least that's what I kept telling the others."

At every stop, they heard doubts from the press and the fans. They heard questions like: "Who would want to watch a tournament with just *women* playing?"

King was also playing great tennis on the tour. She won eight of the fourteen tournaments and earned $37,000 in prize money during the tour's 3½ months.

During one event in St. Petersburg, Florida, she advanced to the semifinals against a 16-year-old Florida high school student named Chris Evert. In the heat of the Florida sun, King became ill and had to **default**. So the first meeting of two American tennis greats was hardly an historic one.

Their second meeting was more important. It came during the semifinals of the 1971 U.S. Open. King felt the match was crucial not only for winning the tournament, but also for keeping fans interested in her Virginia Slims tour. King had already lost at Wimbledon to Evonne Goolagong, an Australian teenager, and another loss to a teenager might turn the public's interest to the younger players instead of the more established ones like King. A loss to Evert could set back the progress the women's tour had already made.

As the two walked onto the stadium court at Forest Hills, New York, they were a study in contrasts. Even at sixteen, Evert was already the calm, stone-faced player the world would come to know. The fiery King psyched herself up by talking to herself and slapping her thighs in anticipation.

In the first game Evert came back from a 0–40 deficit to win the game, and the crowd went crazy. King started executing a perfect game plan, varying the pace, depth, and spin of her shots so Evert couldn't get into a rhythm. After splitting six games in the first set, Evert finally broke down, losing a long backcourt **rally** when King hit a perfect **drop shot**. King won the first set 6–3 and the second 6–2. She later beat Rosie Casals, one of the primary forces in the Virginia Slims tour, in the finals; it was King's second U.S. Open title. More important, tennis fans saw that the older women weren't ready to give up yet; they were still the best in the world.

In the fall Virginia Slims season, King won eleven of the fifteen tournaments and became the first woman athlete ever to earn $100,000 in a year. Reaching that milestone created a lot of publicity for women's tennis and for King. She was in demand for interviews and kept up a busy schedule.

After a brief slump at the beginning of 1972, King was back in form by summer. She won her first French Open. She beat Goolagong in the finals at Wimbledon for her fourth singles title there. Back at Forest Hills for the U.S. Open, she breezed through the competition without losing a set. For her efforts both on the court and in promoting women's tennis in 1972, King was the first woman named Sportsperson of the Year by *Sports Illustrated* magazine.

The success of women's tennis irritated those who believed that women were *not* the equal of men, and therefore shouldn't get equal prize money, or equal media coverage, or equality of any kind. Representing this view in 1973 was a fifty-five-year-old former Wimbledon and U.S. national champion named Bobby Riggs. He was a clever player with a large ego and a flair for self-promotion.

All during his career, Riggs was known in the tennis world for the crazy challenges he would issue to other players. Usually he would offer to play a less talented opponent and then give himself a handicap of some kind. For example, he would sometimes set up chairs on his side of the court. Once Riggs even played a match while holding a dog on a leash.

Early in the year, he began speaking out against women's tennis. He claimed that no woman professional could win more than a game or two from a good male player. He first issued a challenge to King, but she turned him down. She didn't think women's tennis or she herself had anything much to gain by the match.

Another player, Margaret Court, agreed to Riggs's challenge, and after presenting her with flowers before the match, he beat her soundly, 6–2, 6–1. Then King knew she had to play him to prove the worth of women's tennis.

They scheduled the match for Houston's Astrodome. "The Battle of the Sexes," as it was billed, awarded $100,000 to the winner. Over thirty thousand people attended the match and over fifty million watched on television. People who had never seen a tennis match before were tuning in. The opinion of the whole nation about the quality of women's tennis was riding on the match.

When the match began, King knew she had to be aggressive and not allow Riggs an

Trophies were less important to King than equality and fairness.

the set, which ended at 6–4 when he **double-faulted** on set point.

The next two sets were all King. She won them 6–3, 6–3.

Of the match's effect on tennis, King had this to say: "That one event helped put women's tennis on the map and lifted all of tennis to a whole new level of acceptance, introducing the sport to millions who had never before followed it."

To help negotiate with promoters and television networks who became interested in the women's game after King's win, she and other leading women in the game formed the Women's Tennis Association (now the Women's International Tennis Association). As members of a unified group, the women professionals had more power. King was the group's first president.

In 1973, King was at the peak of her career. She won another U.S. Open title in 1974 and one more Wimbledon title in 1975, but younger players like Evert and Martina Navratilova were beginning to dominate the major tournaments.

She continued to play through the 1970s and into the 1980s, winning her last major title in 1980 when she teamed with Navratilova for the women's doubles championship at the U.S. Open. In the decade since then, she has become a tireless booster for the idea of team tennis, where men and women are members of the same

ounce of hope. The first set, she figured, was the most important. If she won it, then he would have to play four sets of tennis to win, and she suspected he would tire out.

With games at 2–2 in the first set, Riggs broke King's serve and took a 3–2 lead. King knew that she would have to break right back in order to deflate his confidence. She was surprised at how slow he was and how weak his serve was. He put a lot of spin on it, but it wasn't anything that King couldn't handle. She broke back to even the set at 3–3.

Court had told her that his **backhand** was not very strong, so when she approached the net, she hit to his backhand side. His backhand passing shots couldn't get by her, and she dominated the rest of

FOR THE EXTRA POINT

Hahn, James and Hahn, Lynn. *King! The Sports Career of Billie Jean King*. Mankato, Minnesota: Crestwood House, 1981.

King, Billie Jean, with Chapin, Kim. *Billie Jean*. New York: Harper & Row, 1974. (Advanced readers.)

King, Billie Jean, with Deford, Frank. *Billie Jean*. New York: Viking Press, 1982. (Advanced readers.)

team. In 1984, she became the first women commissioner of a professional sports league when she was named to head Domino's Pizza Team/Tennis.

Whatever she has devoted herself to, King has always given 100 percent. In 1979 she teamed with Navratilova to win the women's doubles championship at Wimbledon, which gave her a record twenty titles. She broke the record of nineteen, which was held by Elizabeth Ryan. Ryan, who died at age eighty-seven the day before King's victory, had said of King: "Records are made to be broken. If mine has to go, I would like Billie Jean to have it, because she has so much guts." That fighting spirit allowed King not only to win tennis tournaments, but also to take a stand and right the wrongs she saw in tennis. No one in the game has done more.

Even beyond the peak of her career in the 1980s, King remained a competitive player.

BILLIE JEAN KING

CAREER TITLES IN MAJOR TOURNAMENTS

The Lawn Tennis Championships
Wimbledon, England

Singles: 1966–68, 1972, 1973, 1975
Doubles: 1961, 1962, 1965, 1967, 1968, 1970–73, 1979
Mixed Doubles: 1967, 1971, 1973, 1974

The U.S. Open
Forest Hills, New York

Singles: 1967, 1971, 1972, 1974
Doubles: 1964, 1967, 1974, 1978, 1980
Mixed Doubles: 1967, 1971, 1973, 1976

Australian Open
Melbourne, Australia

Singles: 1968

French Open
Paris, France

Singles: 1972
Mixed Doubles: 1967, 1970

OTHER TITLES

Italian Open, Singles: 1970
Italian Open, Doubles: 1970
German Open, Singles: 1970
Virginia Slims Circuit events: 29 titles from 1970–1978

MEMBER OF U.S. TEAMS

Wightman Cup: 1961–67, 1970, 1977, 1978
Federation Cup: 1963–67, 1976–79

INDEX

New York City, 13, 18
New York Coast Guard, 18
Nile River (Egypt), 15-16
Nome (Alaska), 35, 40, 42, 44
North Bimini Island (Bahamas), 20
Norton Sound (Alaska), 42-43
Notre Dame University, 27
Nyad, Aristotle Zason, 13
Nyad, Diana, 13-21
    Bahamas to Florida swim, 20-21
    childhood, 13-14
    college years, 14-15
    Cuba to U.S. swim, 19-20
    heart disease, 14
    Lake Ontario crossing, 17
    school, 13
    statistics, 21
    swim around Manhattan, 18
    training, 16

O'Brien, Ron, 5, 6, 8, 9
Officer's Candidate School, 25
Ohio Wesleyan University, 27
Olympic Games, 14, 48
    Berlin, 24
    boycott, 6
    Los Angeles, 7-8
    Montreal, 3, 4
    Moscow, 6
    Seoul, 1, 8-9
Olympics, Junior, 3
Ontario, Lake, 15, 17
Ortegosa Beach (Cuba), 13, 19
Osmar, Tim, 40
Other Shores (book), 14, 17
Owens, Jesse, 24

Paige, Satchel (Leroy), 26
Pan American Games, 5, 7
Parana River (Argentina), 15
Pasadena (California), 24
Pasadena Junior College, 25
Philadelphia Phillies, 23, 31
Pike (diving), 1, 3, 6
Pittsburgh Crawfords, 26
Platform (diving), 3, 5-6
Preliminary round (diving), 1, 3

Race across Alaska (book), 39, 41, 42
Racism, 24-33
Rainy Pass (Alaska), 39, 40
Rally (tennis), 48, 53
Reader's Digest (magazine), 2
Richards, Bob, 48
Rickey, Branch, 23, 27, 28, 30

Riddles, Libby, 35-45
    childhood, 36
    Iditarod performance, 45
    injury, 41
Riggs, Bobby, 53, 54
Robinson, Jackie, 23-33
    childhood, 24
    college years, 25
    military service, 25-26
    statistics, 33
Robinson, Mack, 24-25
Robinson, Mallie, 24
Robinson, Rachel, 29
Rookie of the Year (award), 32
Rose, Mervyn, 50
Roster (baseball), 26, 31
Rotation (diving), 3
Runner (sled dog racing), 37, 39
Rust, Art, 29
Ryan, Elizabeth, 55

Sanford (Florida), 29
Serve (tennis), 48, 50
Service toss (tennis), 48, 50
Set (tennis), 48, 50
Shark cage (swimming), 19
Shortstop, 26
Siberian husky, 36
Sled dog racing
    dogs, 36
    history, 35-36
    strategy, 36
    terminology, 37
Sneed, Diana *see* Nyad, Diana
South Bend (Indiana), 27
Soviet Union, 5, 36
The Sporting News (magazine), 32
Sports Illustrated (magazine), 5, 6, 9, 15, 53
Springboard (diving), 3
Stanky, Eddie, 32
St. Cloud (Minnesota), 36
St. Louis Browns, 27
St. Louis Cardinals, 27
St. Petersburg (Florida), 52
Strike zone (baseball), 26, 29
Sukeforth, Clyde, 27
Summers, Byron, 18
Support boat (swimming), 14, 15
Swenson, Rick, 40, 41
Swimming Hall of Fame, 15
Swimming, terminology, 14

Tan Liangde, 8
Tennis
    court surfaces, 49
    terminology, 48

Thomas, Charley, 27
Tower (diving), 3, 6
Trot (sled dog racing), 37, 43
Tuck (diving), 3, 4

University of California at Irvine, 6
University of California at Los Angeles (UCLA), 25
University of Miami, 5
University of Missouri, 25
U.S. Clay Court Championships, 51
U.S. Indoor Championships (diving), 5, 8
U.S. Lawn Tennis Association (USLTA), 50, 51, 52
U.S. National Champions, 50
U.S. Open, 51, 52-53, 53, 54
U.S. Outdoors Championships (diving), 5, 6
U.S. Tennis Association *see* U.S. Lawn Tennis Association

Virginia Slims, 51, 53

Wake (swimming), 14, 15
Walker, Dixie, 32
Wheel dog (sled dog racing), 37, 41
Wightman Cup (tennis), 49, 50
Wimbledon, 49, 50, 51, 54, 55
Women's Tennis Association, 54
World Aquatic Championships (diving), 5
World Cup (diving), 6, 7
World Series (baseball), 28
World University Games, 6
World War II, 25

Xiong Ni, 8, 9